MW00768494

WANTED

WANTED

R. DALE WATKINS

Copyright © 2021 by R. Dale Watkins
Published by Clay Bridges in Houston, TX
www.ClayBridgesPress.com

All rights reserved. No part of this publication may be reproduced, stored in a retrieval system, or transmitted in any form by any means, electronic, mechanical, photocopy, recording, or otherwise, with the prior permission of the publisher, except as provided for by USA copyright law.

All Scripture quotations, unless otherwise indicated, are taken from the Holy Bible, New International Version®, NIV®. Copyright ©1973, 1978, 1984, 2011 by Biblica, Inc.™ Used by permission of Zondervan. All rights reserved worldwide. The "NIV" and "New International Version" are trademarks registered in the United States Patent and Trademark Office by Biblica, Inc.™

ISBN: 978-1-953300-35-5 (Paperback)
ISBN: 978-1-953300-49-2 (Hardback)
eISBN: 978-1-953300-36-2

Sales: Most Clay Bridges titles are available in special quantity discounts.

Custom imprinting or excerpting can also be done to fit special needs. Contact Clay Bridges at Info@ClayBridgesPress.com.

CONTENTS

FOREWORD

By "Stephen"

This book captures the tragic, unbearable, pure torment of my upbringing, told from my brother's perspective. However, more strikingly, it is an unexpected story of redemption and hope, culminating in the discovery of what it means to be authentically, passionately Wanted.

But Wanted is not only my story or even my brother's story. It is the story of a mother desperately caught in her own darkness and uncontrollably inflicting her desperation on her children. It is the story of a father unable to face the weighty reality of what had become his life, choosing instead to run away, leaving chaos and neglect in his wake. It is the story of four children trying to navigate the chronically horrible environment that is their home, blinking through the daily tears, and trying, with no hope of success, to find some sense of self-worth, security, and love. In it, you just might find your story.

One day not too long ago, decades after the timetable of this book, I was sitting on the couch in my family room feeling a bit thirsty. Gathered with me in front of the television were my beautiful wife and five amazing children. All of us were laughing through a hilarious episode of "America's Funniest Home Videos." I got up to get a glass of water in the kitchen. As I re-entered the family room, fully enjoying the laughter, I was suddenly stopped – like a hand had reached out and was pressing into my chest. I could not move forward. Then, His sweet whisper spoke to me as clear as day, "Look around, my son. Try and think of a single thing that was stolen from you when you were a child that I have not replaced." I was shaken, but I obeyed.

I thought carefully. There amid the laughing and silliness, tears came to my eyes. As I reflected on my life, I suddenly had a profound revelation of how meticulously God had worked, like a proficient, engrossed, skilled Craftsman, to attend to and restore His son.

The stories told in these pages must be told, not because of their drama (however compelling) or only to provide a window into the real-life brutality of child abuse (as important as that may be). They must shine a light of hope for all who will read it whose hope has been lost.

My prayer is that you will find yourself in these pages: in the despair of the seemingly impossible life-realities of a mother and father; in Anne's desperate desire to please; in Dan's attempts to be strong despite his overwhelming feelings of inadequacy; in my futile wishes for a better tomorrow; in the author's crushing desire to be Wanted; and in his ultimate discovery that he always was!

Arise, shine;

For your light has come!

And the glory of the Lord is risen upon you.

For behold, the darkness shall cover the earth,

And deep darkness the people;

But the Lord will arise over you,

And His glory will be seen upon you. (Isaiah 60:1-2 NIV)

The Fierce Storm

I awakened in that cold, leather recliner in the hospital room, next to Mom. The wind rattled against the large window and seeped through the cracks of the windowsill on this chilly February morning. I pulled the blanket a little closer to my shoulders to cover my whole body. It had been a long night.

Mom had been brought to the hospital early yesterday because she complained of leg pain. I had delayed coming until around noon because I was annoyed by her list of complaints. When I arrived at her new residence, where she had moved just five days earlier, I was startled by what I found. Mom was on her queen-sized bed, apparently unable to move her right leg. It was all she could do to try to lift it. I checked her vital signs and asked her about pain. Everything seemed to be normal, except it clearly was not.

As I walked through her residence, I saw evidence of her long battle with Irritable Bowel Syndrome (IBS). It had left its mark throughout the whole apartment, staining many of the surfaces in her home. The stench in her apartment wreaked, and the place where she had come to rest on her bed was unsightly.

Mom ached in what was obviously a prolonged state of pain. Quivering, she spoke in a somber and low tone: "My leg! Oh, my leg!" Yet, there was nothing definitively wrong. It baffled me until I gave up trying to find an answer and resolved to call the ambulance.

Now, I got up from the vinyl recliner and checked on Mom. I smiled at her. She smiled back and asked for me to look up. I followed her request, turning my head, and looking at the tile that spread across the ceiling of her hospital room. She seemed to be pointing to a specific tile, where she was clearly seeing something that was not visible.

"Look!" she said, "Furry, white kittens. They are looking straight at me." Her smile was contagious, but my bewilderment caused my eyebrows to rise, and my eyes rolled as I tried to keep my chuckle hidden. Mom has gone nutty, I thought to myself. The moment stayed with me, though.

My wife and I had taken Mom in two years earlier. Her throat cancer had spread throughout her whole body. At the time, it looked as if her time was coming to an end quickly. The decision to bring her into our home was the hardest thing I had to do. To expose my children and wife to the narcissistic, self-absorbed, and controlling person that Mom was, and still is, stressed me to no end.

As the weeks and months passed with her living with us, her cancer stopped growing and the doctors went into a "watch and wait" pattern. Mom took it to mean her cancer was gone completely. This false narrative made her challenging to deal with when it came to facing other medical issues. Her IBS, only diagnosed two months before this hospital stay, was the cause of her constant diarrhea over the last couple of years.

Mom had always been a very difficult woman to be around. My motives in taking her in were to give her a home, a genuine family atmosphere, something she rarely experienced in her life. My intention was also to take care of her every need, no matter what it would cost us. Unfortunately, the cost was much more than I imagined, but not financially. Rather, the weight of Mom's presence in our home came to be a very heavy burden.

When we moved Mom into her own place five days ago, her exhausting, controlling nature within our home finally had its end. We found this beautiful apartment that she could call her own. She was happy, as was my family now that she had her own residence.

The doctors ran all kinds of tests to determine Mom's condition while she was in the emergency room. All the tests were negative. However, two things caused the doctors to move her to a room where she would stay overnight: Her chest x-ray came back, showing a dark circle within her lungs, and her blood pressure and heart rate were quite low. So, they kept her in the hospital to keep an eye on her. Otherwise, they would have been ready to release her. With that assurance, the doctor had expressed hope that she would be going home soon. His words brought me calm in this uncertainty.

Sleeping in that recliner had made my back sore. Yet I sat in it again now and reflected on Mom's startling choice from yesterday. While in the emergency room, I had stepped away to grab a bite to eat. A record-keeping assistant had come in to gather information from Mom, who had been fully cognizant and answered all his questions amiably. He was gone by the time I got back to her room. She had summarized the visit with these words, "He asked if I wanted to be resuscitated if my heart stopped. I told him no!" She had spoken in a quiet, confident, almost eerie tone. Now the words repeated themselves over and over in my head.

My daydreaming stopped. Looking over at her, I saw that Mom had fallen back asleep. Her vital signs were still well below normal. I was getting concerned, but took it all in stride, trusting the doctors every step of the way.

My mind wandered again. I began to reflect on the third reason that I had brought Mom to live with us. Many had questioned my decision. Nevertheless, I knew it was what

I was supposed to do. I wanted her to experience the same spiritual awakening I had. I wanted the same for all those I knew and met, especially for my family. My heart was hurting for Mom, both for her frail state now and for her broken heart all those years ago.

Yet, she was not the only one who pained my heart. My story is just a story, I mused to myself, like any other. Yet, I knew it was so much more. I had been wrestling with writing my family's narrative for six years now. Nevertheless, as Mom lay in that bed, the need had become very apparent and even more urgent that I finish what I set out to do.

The storms of life are vicious and ferocious at times. I wanted my mother to have peace as I have come to intimately know it. For that matter, I long for anyone who struggles with the tortuous nature of this life, with the storms that seem to have no end, and who does not know peace, to know there is freedom, a way out, and life on the other side. It is why I must tell my story…

CHAPTER ONE
Surprise!

"Oh yes, you shaped me first inside, then out; you formed me in my mother's womb. I thank you, High God – you're breathtaking! Body and soul, I am marvelously made! I worship in adoration – what a creation! You know me inside and out, you know every bone in my body; You know exactly how I was made, bit by bit, how I was sculpted from nothing into something. Like an open book, you watched me grow from conception to birth; all the stages of my life were spread out before you. The days of my life were all prepared before I'd even lived one day."

(Psalm 39:13-16 MSG)

She leaned over the vanity and stared into the mirror. All that would come were tears and they would not stop. A bevy of emotions flooded her!

She had taken the day off from her rather new job, the first one she had since her vows were spoken. A couple of days earlier, she had noticed that her cycle had come and gone without anything happening. Now she was scared to go to the doctor, but what choice did she have?

The doctor's team tried to calm and comfort Mom, but she would not have any of it. She had just received the news that I was sitting in her belly, six weeks into her first trimester. What was she to do? The tears came even more fiercely.

Outside her bathroom door that evening was her husband of eleven years stretched out on the bed after having been gone most of the day. His return, after running out on the family, had been only a short while ago. While away, he had met another lady, and the fling turned into a full-blown affair.

He had come to despise Mom, and finances had also taken their toll. As a result, he took a second lien on our home and filed bankruptcy shortly before walking back into the lives of his wife and three kids. It was his guilt, as he remembered his mother's admonition and his family's spurning of him, that finally wore on him. So, he came home to try to make a go of it.

That painful recollection now gave Mom's tears pause, and anger flooded her. As quietly as she could, she cursed at her lying, deceitful husband from behind the door. Then she looked down at her stomach as the silent tears turned to weeping. How was she going to tell him?

Still madly in love with him, Mom knew that the years of their constant yelling, his disappearing until late at night, his silent treatments, and his love of music—but not of her—had left their mark on her heart. He had walked out, leaving her to pick up everything and start a new career while trying to feed and raise three kids. She did not know whether to feel outrage or relief when he came back home.

Her world had blown up when he left the family with no thought of returning. The anger and rage she felt toward him turned to violence towards the kids, especially the youngest of the three, Stephen. Dad had noticed all this upon his return. There was not much he could say or do because of his own guilt. Sensing that he already knew about the goings-on during his absence, she still felt compelled to hide it from him at all costs, which she became a master at doing. It seemed to be working, she thought to herself, with him back home and all. The two of them seemed to be able to make things work for a little while. It is hard to say they enjoyed each other's company, but Dad tried to be a dad.

Now, her shameful memories stopped, and her panic about the news of a new child tore at her. As her rage with my dad set in as well, she grabbed at her tummy, wishing to tear me out. Still hiding in the bathroom, she sat down on the toilet seat. Her rage subsided, but shame cuddled up right beside her.

She remembered following her own dad around every golf course he designed, his passion for golf architecture evident. She would be on the grounds or even nearby, but she could not come close to seeing what he poured himself into. Whether her pain was noticeable to him she did not know, but she constantly fought for his attention. Meanwhile, his eighteen-hour days on the golf course undermined her individuality, maturity, and character. Although she was captivated by his love for the art of the game, all his love was left on the golf landscape. When his time came, he died suddenly from a heart attack on one of his amazing golf masterpieces, as he walked the terrain. Mom was sixteen.

Mom's reminiscences turned from years gone by to times not so long ago. Her husband had fallen in love with music and percussion. Together, they ran a music store, and he would spend all day, every day at that store. It was all he wanted, and it was his way to get away from the yelling and screaming he encountered when he came home in the evenings. She sought his love just as she had craved her dad's love, but he, too, neglected and abandoned her, only with much more guile and intent. Dad's beloved music store went under shortly before his departure.

Her face was cupped in her hands now, despair setting in like a ball and chain around her neck. She began to weigh her options. Their financial mess was deeply stressing Mom, even before she knew I was to come. She despised the thought of government help, because of her staunch British upbringing, so she was determined to make things work.

Yet Mom had always resented doing the finances for the bookstore, after having watched her own mom do bookkeeping for three decades. This left her with an ire toward my dad, feeling that he owed her for even attempting to run the money side of the store, not to mention the upkeep of the house and kids as well. Adding to her stress was the fact that both she and my dad spent money impulsively and irresponsibly. As a result, tempers flared perpetually before his exit. The bills came due, and their marriage hung in the balance.

By the time my dad returned, the money problems were glaring, much worse than they had ever been before. He found himself in a deeper financial hole than when he had left. Although Dad was a brilliant businessman with the heart of an artist, the bankruptcy left them with nothing after the business was disbanded and sold for scraps. While his artistic and analytical wisdom were stellar, he lacked any wisdom at all in his personal life. Without that ability to navigate adult responsibilities, a rage devoured him, causing him to stiff-arm anyone offering him guidance, and with no one to offer him help, Dad then floundered. Fleeing conflict, he caused our family to crumble and implode.

Mom looked down at her abdomen again from her bent position. Panic began to take over as she thought about the cost of another mouth to feed. Yet her financial worry quickly gave way to a much graver terror, and it struck Mom hard. She stood up suddenly because she could not stay still. She began pacing and talking incessantly to herself. The same tormented thought came over and over: "What if I lose him again?" Despite all the problems in her marriage, she worried that this pregnancy might cost her her marriage.

Stopping in front of the mirror, she looked deeply into the eyes reflected at her. The new terror formulated into a sinister plan. She gathered herself, disguising her red cheeks and puffy eyes with make-up, swallowing the onset of fears from the ongoing heartache. She put on a light fragrance to lighten the mood.

Reaching for the handle, Mom opened the door smoothly. She stepped into the bedroom. Dad's eyes noticed her but did not acknowledge her presence. Walking around to her side of the bed, she slid under the covers. As if she were confident of the new plan she had conceived, she looked over his way. With no evidence of the bathroom meltdown, she said, "I went to the doctor today." Dad kept the paper in front of him, deep in silence.

She got closer and reached down to look over his paper. His agitation was growing. She noticed and went on, "You and I are expecting again!" He looked at her in surprise but did not say anything. As he made his way to the door, she got out of bed, noticing his displeasure with the news. She cut him off before he could leave. Weaponizing her words, she shouted at him, "Well, you have put us in this position. You ran out on us!"

His anger became visible. She did not care because she was determined to make him feel the pain that my existence would bring to them. The yelling and screaming went deep into the night until Dad slammed the door behind him and headed to the car.

Returning the next morning, he knew the beginning of the end was here.

CHAPTER TWO

Vanished

"For the Lord will not reject his people, he will never forsake his inheritance."

(Psalm 94:14 NIV)

"Lord, do not abandon me, do not stand at a distance, my God. Come quickly to help me, my Lord and my savior."

(Psalm 38:21,22 NLT)

Mom got up and prepared herself for work. Dad was already downstairs, messing with something in the garage.

My three older siblings, Ann, Dan, and Stephen were ten, nine, and six years old, respectively. Ann was a bright, gregarious young lady, who was as tall as her gorgeous blonde locks were long. Dan, diagnosed as underdeveloped at an early age, had dark brown, curly hair and a strong upper torso. He made up for his "slowness" by learning to be crafty and shifty.

Stephen, a slight, blonde boy, was a bundle of energy, who was often overlooked among his brother and sister.

All had learned from an early age that if they wanted Mom's or Dad's attention, they had to fight for it. That fight was not just with each parent but with each other as well. This caused chaos along with terror in all of them, always having to wrestle for their parent's love and attention. When that attention was found, it often was not an affectionate and nurturing moment. Rather, it was in servitude and oppression that each child found attention, and only the needs of the adults mattered.

After I was born, Ann ran to my crib and gave me attention at the least sound of a cry. She would have already prepared the bottle, forcing it into my mouth before anyone shouted at her to do so. Mom would come into the living room and head towards the front door. She rarely said goodbye before she left for work, but the echo of the slamming door gave notice to everyone in the house that she was gone.

That was the sound Dad had been waiting for on this day. He fought off the anxiousness, and little excitement, that erupted within him. He had come to a decision in the last couple of days. Regardless, he reconciled to himself, there was no other option! He headed to the bedroom and labored vigorously, getting his things together behind the closed door.

Living in the foothills of the Rockies, the air was light and fresh. When the snow came, it was dry and fluffy. Sun rays were warming as they hit our shoulders. Now, watching the rays come through the window, Dad shifted his focus from packing to reflect on the visit from his mom. She had made the twenty-five-mile trek south to visit a couple of weeks before.

Prior to her visit, he shrewdly went on one of his late rendezvous away from the house. Dad willingly deceived Mom about his disappearances, so Mom was unaware of his trysts. Nevertheless, he met Jo, his estranged lover from the original separation a year before. They recently had begun seeing each other again.

When Jo saw Dad's exasperation, she knew something was different. She had had enough of his games, his pretending to keep his broken family together. Plus, she wanted him for herself. So, Dad suggested to Jo, "What if we split up the kids? We can take Ann and Stephen with us, and Dan and the baby stay with her." A grin came over her face. Those were the words she had longed for, even if it meant that she had to be a stepmom.

He paused in his contemplation as he shifted bags, clothes, and belongings to the car. Back in his room, he retrieved some old music items to take with him, all while remembering the courage it had taken to face his mom and his wife together.

He had proposed a plan that would shift the course of our family forever. It all seemed to be a reasonable strategy for him.

Dad's memories flashed back to his mom's visit. He shifted in his seat. The air in the room became tense and hard to breathe. Ann swiftly hauled me to the basement while the boys went outside to play.

Grandma Lila was short, with gleaming, gray hair that settled on her shoulders. After her husband's drinking and verbal abuse had run its course, he had divorced her. She then leaned on her strong-chin heritage and raised her two boys with an undeterred, firm Christian hand. She had always been tough on her youngest son, and she could tell he was nervous that day.

Dad could feel the frog in his throat. His lifestyle and choices had always shamed him in front of his mom. That was small compared to what he was about to suggest, a solution that went against the fabric of the way he was brought up. He knew he was leaving, but it was just a matter of saying when and with whom. This conversation was not merely important; it was necessary.

"It's time for me to go!" he had announced abruptly. "This self-absorbed, crazy woman (Mom) has tested me to my wit's end. I will take Ann and Stephen, and I will leave Dan and Dale."

Grandma Lila had stood straight up, almost hyperventilating from the words coming from her son. Mom had grizzled with fret that turned to anger. She was astonished by her husband's words, and even more so by her mother-in-law's wrath. It was the first time she had seen this woman come to her defense.

"Now I know you two have not had it easy, but this is just nonsense!" Grandma Lila continued, "You have already disappeared for almost a year, and now, here you are, proposing a preposterous brainstorm. You have failed in your duty as a husband and father, and now you want to separate these four?" She pointed around the room wildly. "I will not have it!" She paused as if to say more, but that was all that came. So, she sat down. That is when Mom stepped in and began yelling with frantic hysteria. And Dad walked out.

Now, rattled by the boys' noise as they played outside, these remembrances vanished from his mind. He shouted their names in his strong baritone voice. Everything came to an instant stillness. He finished packing and moved the rest of his things to his car, parked out on the street. Dan and Stephen watched as if in slow-motion. Ann climbed the stairs with me in her arms, clinging to her. She stared at Dad's movements. The boys' mouths hung open. As the last bag was pitched into the trunk, he marched back into the house. It was becoming clear that this was the last time they would see their father.

Dad motioned to Ann to come downstairs to the basement. She put me down in front of my brothers and followed swiftly. He looked into her eyes, for she was Daddy's girl, or so she thought, and he said goodbye. He went on to ask her to take care of her brothers. She piped up with the brightest grin, and proudly responded to his directive, "Of course I will." She loved that she was commissioned, and she knew that the responsibilities of the house were in her hands now. A tear rolled down her cheek. Dad wiped it away, kissed her on the forehead, and headed back upstairs.

As Ann reached the top of the staircase, she picked me back up. Dad had already walked out the front door. Dan was now at the top of the driveway. Stephen followed Dad out the screen door as it swung shut on him, slipping out just before it hit him. Ann held me in her arms as she gazed out through the mesh wire. Dad quickly made it around to the driveway where he found Dan. He quietly spoke to him: "Keep your chin up." Putting his right palm on Dan's head, Dad rumpled his hair and then kept moving.

As he reached the car door, Dad opened it and sat down, putting the key in the ignition. Before he started the car, for the first time, he turned around and looked at Stephen, who was sitting on the bottom step of the porch. Stephen's hands rested in his palms until Dad's eyes met his, and they stared at each other for more than a moment. Stephen was in utter disbelief, feeling lost.

Dad turned his gaze down the street that he would never drive down again. He started the car, shifted the gears, and drove away.

I was two months old.

CHAPTER THREE
Soul Starved

"I am the Bread of Life."

(John 6:35 AMP)

"I am the Light of the World."

(John 8:12 AMP)

"I am the Door."

(John 10:9 AMP)

"I am the Good Shepherd."

(John 10:11 AMP)

"I am the Resurrection and the Life."

(John 11:25 AMP)

"I am the [only] Way [to God] and the [real] Truth
and the [real] Life."

(John 14:6 AMP)

"I am the Vine."

(John 15:5 AMP)

I was laying on the cold, tile floor in the master bathroom. My pouting about the poop I had just released irritated Mom. Having sat in it, my cloth diaper stuck to my backside. Mom lifted my legs and, peeling off the diaper, grabbed the soapy rag, and wiped my bottom.

She yelled out Ann's name several times, but there was not an instant response. Her irritation turned to annoyance. Meanwhile, my hunger rumbled, changing my pouting to a muffled cry. Mom cussed at me as she hand-washed the diaper in the sink.

She continued to yell for Ann. There was still no response. Walking out of the bathroom, Mom threw the diaper towards the dirty clothes, to be hung up to dry later. She did not return quickly. The longer she stayed away, the louder my cry became. Still, Mom did not respond. Instead, I could hear her in the bedroom: "God damn it, you son-of-a-bitch!"

Then, alone and unattended, I could no longer hear Mom. Shivering on the tile floor, my movements were only enough to wiggle from side to side. I screamed out as loud as I could, but no one came. My bawling convulsed into a frightened tremble, and I shrieked uncontrollably.

Mom's moment away turned into several minutes without her reappearing. Suddenly, a centipede came out of the wall to investigate. It came close, touching my skin. When my shrill cry screeched down the hallway and into the other rooms, the critter went away as fast as it came.

I started coughing and choking, able to catch my breath only for a second at a time. Phlegm built up on my vocal cords again. I started gasping between coughing spurts. Choking was taking my breath away. I coughed repeatedly and relentlessly. Finally, my lungs cleared. My shrieks vibrated and echoed off the floor.

Mom entered the room, her agitation gone. Now her anger burst through her neck veins instead. She reached for me and held me like a sack of potatoes between her hands. Shaking me, her violent thrusts silenced my shrieks. As she stopped, her "angry face"—clenched teeth with her lips pointing northeast—melted into uncertainty. Her quietness was eerie. I began to shiver in her arms. Mom was lost in her own thoughts, and every effort to calm me was useless. The coldness of the room added to my shivers until my body shuddered wildly.

Even in her arms, I was unaided and alienated from her. Mom stepped out of the bathroom, carrying me into her bedroom. She placed me on the bed and just stared at me from her standing position. I calmed down enough to see her eyes. They were cold and hard to look into. Mom pulled a shirt over my head and fastened a new cloth diaper onto me.

Running into the room, Ann apologized profusely. Mom gave her a dirty look, turning back towards me and waving her hands in the air as though she had given up. A sour face came over me. I wanted to cry but nothing came out. Walking out of the room to get a drink, Mom looked back at me. Disdain oozed from her like sweat.

Ann picked me up and cradled me. Stepping out of Mom's room into hers, the quiet tone of her singing was enough to put my body at ease as she sat on her bed. I finally rested and fell asleep in her arms.

Ann laid me in my crib in her room. Then Mom scolded her for hours, blaming her for the suffering, irritations, and pressure Mom felt she was under constantly. She slapped Ann once or twice, as though my sister deserved it. After all, it was all her fault, right? It made no difference that it was not; Ann carried it as such, and the guilt laid its wound deep within her.

Mom finally let Ann head to bed. I saw her walk into the room as the light from the hallway awakened me. Ann crawled under her covers and looked over at me. Our eyes met. The tenderness from her eyes warmed my heart, and my cooing warmed hers. My eleven-year-old sister had become my maternal love.

Any affection received from Mom was disjointed and disconnected. My body developed, yet my soul's growth was stunted. My thoughts rambled and raced irrationally, my emotions froze in time, my nerves shuttered, and my consciousness became comatose. With my heart callousing, I was learning to become cold and distant as I mimicked Dad's desertion and abandonment, along with Mom's disengaged social-wiring and painful yearning to belong, not trusting anyone.

On the other hand, my smile and infectious energy lightened the intensity of the family. Everyone was tender towards me even if it was not evident. When the atmosphere was fracked with force by high pressures of violence or cruelty, my family saw to it that I was sheltered and safeguarded. If things lightened, I became the entertainment. I craved the attention when it came. Dan watched and laughed at my silliness. Stephen wrestled me into tickling fits. Ann was my shelter and rest. Mom was even caught smiling at times towards me.

In an awfully long and hard hurricane known as my family's upbringing, my young presence brought a hope and a lightness to life. In paradoxical reasoning, each one of my siblings wanted to give me a sense of childhood normalcy. Such an ingenuous thought surrendered as each had to fight for his or her own survival daily. Meanwhile, my soul

starved from the hidden destitution that was in the moment
and to come.

I was eighteen months old.

CHAPTER FOUR
Unwanted

"When my father and my mother have forsaken me,
then doth JEHOVAH gather me."

(Psalm 27:10 YLT1898)

T he war between enmities (Mom and Dad) was over, but the devastation was just beginning. Dad's leaving was the explosion that threw everything into a fury. The dizzying days thereafter are difficult to translate into eloquent verbiage. Nothing was certain, except that Dad was gone!

Although Ann made sure the house ran as smoothly as possible, she became a puppet and busy body. She was Mom's pull-string puppet, yet she relished the role. It gave her significance and made her feel appreciated. She finally felt she was in her element. Over time, though, the role wore her down until she had nothing left to give.

Ann had been Daddy's little girl, and when he shafted the family, she found a new life in serving, giving, and caring for others. She was the glue in the family's survival, but it devastated her inside, leaving her empty and without roots. The result was that, from cooking dinner and balancing the checkbook to doing most of the chores, Ann clearly became Mom's personal slave.

At an early age, Dan had a procedure done to see if he was impeded mentally or physically. Mom took this quite personally. As Dan got older, Mom found herself repeatedly defending him, renouncing pejorative nicknames and negative claims against Dan. Her actions formed a bond between the two of them that the other three children did not share. Yet, it was a very unhealthy mother-and-son relationship.

Dad purposely had been distant from Dan while he was around. The vigorous defense Mom put forth for Dan, along with her strong attachment to him, had caused Dad to separate himself from Dan, isolating himself from any interaction with Dan. When Dad left, Dan became even more clearly Mom's favorite. Ann and Stephen watched Dan do some wicked things and blame them, especially Stephen. Mom seemed not to notice that Dan had a mischievous streak, hence, his crafty and cunning ways were hidden. That is how Dan began to enable Mom's abusive behaviors.

Stephen was a remarkable child mentally. He grasped things very quickly, and life's insights seemed to come easily to him. Since there was never enough to keep him entertained, he investigated anything he could get his hands on. So, Mom considered him a troublemaker and often compared him to our father.

Mom repeatedly reminded Stephen to be still or warned him to get out of her sight as his endless need to be busy became quite annoying. It was for this reason that Stephen became the scapegoat or culprit for the family after Dad left. He had looked up to Dad, but the day our father left him on the porch... well, that tore apart Stephen inside. His curiosity kept the loneliness away, however, it got him in trouble at school and at home. Mom's vehemence toward Dad shifted to Stephen, the one who reminded her of her ex-husband the most. Stephen then became Mom's punching bag.

With Mom already working nights full time, Dad's departure required her to get a second job. However, Dad's trail of damage did not seem to end quickly. After he was gone, the local creditors came demanding payment of the bad debt. Dad had taken the checkbook and written several checks to businesses. He also had taken out loans in addition to the mortgages. There was no money. It was as if the checks were written on paper made of rubber as each check bounced, and the creditors flocked to Mom's door. Mom was threatened and served notice to pay or further action would be taken.

This broke Mom, and she received help in the strangest ways, although government assistance was not one of them. Somehow, these were humiliations she could not accept. The first help came in the form of a caretaker named Ila. She took us in, especially me. I spent much of my time during my young days under her care. She had other kids she watched, especially after school, but Ila prevented me from experiencing much of the danger that began to come from home.

The second help came from a mechanic named Jerry. Mom was lost when it came to cars. Once she found Jerry, he seemed to take a liking to her, and not just compassion, because he noticed her neediness. There was romantic flirting that went on for several years between them. Nobody really knew how serious it was, nor when it was off or on, but nothing really came of it, either. Jerry really came through for Mom, though, and not just with her vehicle. It is suggested that he helped financially and more.

There were other helpers who just seemed to appear as well. People from work stepped in with solutions to Mom's family needs. A pastor at a local church took interest in looking in on us from time to time, especially Ann. Then, there was help from both Grandmas. Dad's Mom visited us often. Mom felt that she owed it to see her, after all, she was the one who kept the family together. Dad's Mom looked after us on several levels. Her heartache from her son and compassion from her beliefs seemed to compel her. Dad's brother and his wife intervened every so often, and some of the most memorable events, like being invited into their home for holidays, lifted our spirits to know that there was life outside our home.

The final help came in the way of Mom's mom. She lived in Washington, D.C., and could not visit often. Her support came mostly from phone calls. However, her checks appeared in our mail. When nobody else could ease or soothe Mom's emotional flareups and temper tantrums, Grandma was the one who spent hours on the phone with her. She was the only one who really knew Mom and was close to her after Dad left.

By all appearances, we were making it work. There were some missed meals, even malnutrition, which could be attributed to a lack of money. However, withholding meals was also a weapon Mom used. She had one rule she lived by financially: She would often say, "we must rob Peter to pay Paul." And it worked for the most part. She was able to keep the money vultures at a distance.

School for the older siblings was a good escape from the dogma of our home. However, it proved to have its own challenges, from bullying to isolation. Each of the kids' grades was good, except for maybe Jim, who seemed to struggle more than the rest of us. By all accounts, we seemed to have a "normal," middle-class home, in terms of society and education, after Dad's departure. Yet, people did seem to notice the stress on the family, which explains why help came unexpectedly. Nevertheless, Mom was applauded by many for her ability to raise four kids, hold down two jobs, and manage the life of a single mother. I give great thanks for her efforts.

Yet Mom was a chameleon. She could change and adapt to almost any situation. She loved to tell stories of her experiences, her dad's accomplishments, her travels and travails with her ex-husband, and about the splendid English ancestry that she came from. She dominated conversations, and most listeners were courteous enough because Mom's stories were appealing and interesting. Folks were especially attentive when there was a commonality between Mom's tales and personal experiences.

Yet very few picked up on the abuse within our home. Mom became amazingly talented on three fronts: deflection, defense, and denial. She kept up appearances as a businesswoman would keep her private life out of her professional life. Appearances were splendid, but the whitewash of the walls on the outside kept the horror on the inside of our home hidden from the public's view.

That first year after Dad left, my first year of life, was like that of ruins after a war zone. Normally, after a war has ended, the people begin to pick up their lives and start again. Although we did pick up our lives, a new war had begun. This war was between Mom's emotional survival and Mom's devastating shame, an internal warzone replete with a minefield and an artillery assault that rained down on her children.

Mom's temper flared randomly, endlessly, and violently. Dad's departure left a cavernous void, filled by Mom's tirades at her children. She spewed threats and railed at their shortcomings. Yet one element was new: Her temper tantrums were followed by extreme violence. What I believe was Mom's attempt to discipline, such as spanking, became more of a tortuous fit of fury.

Ann, Dan, and Stephen were emotionally shattered. The threat of terror froze the occupants of our home with intense anxiety and alarm. Mom's rage lasted for hours at a time, followed by lengthy speeches about how lowly her life had become. Those monologues, after the violence and yelling, would end with us standing on our feet for hours at a time, continuously nodding in agreement at whatever she said. Mom's constant yelling compelled us to agree with her at any cost. Yet there was no way to keep the focus on what she was talking about after four, five, six hours of it, often going on until three or four o'clock in the morning. Because of this, it often stirred her yelling and violence a second or third go-round when we would fail to nod or agree with her, simply because of exhaustion or being lost in a trance.

The relief came in that Mom worked a lot. Between school, Mom's need for sleep, and her third shift of work, we had time between her explosive tantrums. That time was not always a calm time, though. When at school, we dared not get into trouble and let Mom find out about it. We also dared not talk about or show any bruising to school staff.

When Mom was away at work, we knew we had better make sure that the chores were done and that the house was spotless. Even if there were a fingerprint on the wall or a picture out of place, our acute panic would set in, anticipating what could happen. When Mom slept, we dared not wake her as she was an exceptionally light sleeper. The eerie silence in a house that could become chaotic at any given moment, especially when she was awakened, kept us quiet enough to hear a pin drop. The TV or music was just not something you turned on. Any playing was limited by the noise we could make.

The house was usually in one of three states: making sure things were perfect in Mom's absence; making sure things were perfectly still in Mom's presence; or observing Mom's rage, violence, and monologues as they flared. No matter what state, there was one faithful component in the first six or seven years after Dad left: the dread of Mom and what she would do.

My first year of life was protected from much of the abuse. I was either at Ila's or I was in the care of Ann. Ila attended to my needs while I was away from the house, and

Ann was diligently looking after or protecting me while in the house. Yet the yelling and violence took their toll even if I was not in the room. I became known as the "quiet" and "good" baby, never causing havoc.

Three devastations came from that first year, which began the terror that has haunted me. First, the "quiet" baby that I was on the outside was a result of the trauma and shock of my surroundings. Second, Dad's physical abandonment and Mom's emotional abandonment set the tone for the basis of my identity.

The last devastation I was born into was what I have come to realize as one of two key elements in the formation of a healthy and strong child. Mom's need to work, to sleep, and to defend herself for survival left no room for anyone else. This caused everyone else to cower, to acquiesce to her self-absorption.

I was born into a family with a single mom who had no idea how to bond with or to nurture her baby. When I cried, it was Ann who tended to me. When I hungered, it was Ann who fed me. When I just wanted to be held, Mom left me on the floor until Ann came to get me. It is not that Mom did not care, rather, she could not care because her attention was filled by her own neediness.

There was little violence or yelling when I was with her in the presence of others. However, when I was alone with her, I was her pain, her thorn, and not her son. Like a mother cat who abandons her kittens or a mother bird that builds a nest for her little ones only to never return, my needs were forgotten at the more pressing lure of self-absorption and vanity. Whether it was by decision or circumstance, intended or inadvertent, a recurring message was sent to my innermost: I was unwanted.

CHAPTER FIVE

A Day in the Life

"Tell fearful souls, 'Courage! Take heart!' God is here,
right here, on his way to put things right and redress
all wrongs. He's on his way! He'll save you!"

(Isaiah 35:4 MSG)

They were eye to eye. Mom sat up on the couch and looked straight into his eyes with her usual scowl, forehead skin scrunched down, teeth clenched on the left side, and her lips angled upward and to the side. She demanded an answer, but he was out of answers. Stephen's gaze stared into her eyes. He wanted desperately to look away, but he knew the torture would go to another level. Instead, he tried to stay as still as he could, but his body would not obey as it convulsed and shivered from the deep fear he was experiencing.

Stephen tried to tell her the truth, but she was not having it. He tried to stay silent, but that brought on more lashes. Knowing the quickest way out was through lies, he said, "Yes! Yes, I did it!" Pausing for a deep breath, he continued.

"I'm sorry, Mom. I am really sorry." He bent over as much as he could without taking his eyes away from hers. His whole body quaking with sobs, Stephen's knees buckled under the pressure. He fell at her feet.

I sat next to my sister on the couch downstairs, playing with my blocks. This became our haven from these moments. Yet Stephen's sobbing vibrated through the ceiling. Trying to read a book, Ann was not able to concentrate.

Mom waved Dan over to assist with getting Stephen off the floor. He stood and watched outside the kitchen entrance. He tried to disguise himself as though he was not there. His slowness to respond caught Mom's attention. She raised her intensity in her voice, "Get over here and pick him up." He ran quickly scared that he would suffer the same bout of "punishment" that our brother had endured.

Stephen was stretched out on the couch once again. "I guess 100 lashes is not enough for you to learn your lesson! Maybe we need to do another 150. Then, what about the lying? I guess another 150 for that, too." Her son was trying to stretch out as far as he could on his stomach, one hand clenched in the other, and his arms wrapped around his head reaching out as far as he could. He could not stretch out completely, though, because of the severe red welts that covered his lower back, buttocks, and upper thighs.

Mom noticed and got nasty about Stephen's effort. She looked at Dan and spit as she commanded him, "Grab his hands." Dan knew the exercise too well. He looked at Mom and tried to come up with words to stop this, but none came. He reached for Stephen's hands and pulled his arms so that the body was stretched out as far as possible.

Mom grabbed the leather belt off the coffee table, coiled it so that the buckle was showing. She ordered Stephen to count with each whip across his midsection. The strap and buckle flailed away and landed in no particular pattern. Stephen screamed and counted, all in one breath, each lash.

Ann put me on the floor. As she went back to the couch, she buried her head down into the cushion covering her ears as tightly as she could. Once I heard the lashes and screaming from my brother, I looked around, my mouth hanging open. My sister was preoccupied. I wanted to cry, but nothing came. I wanted help, but no one came. So, I grabbed the block and gnawed at it. At least it brought a little comfort.

"One-hundred fifty…" Stephen squeaked out. Dan let go of his hands as he was tearing up, but he knew he could not cry out loud. Stephen buried himself as far into the couch as he could. "Well, maybe you will fess up to leaving the smudge on my wall. You know what I do for you and how hard I work to make sure you eat?! And I come home to see this. Well, if you think horseplay is fun…" Mom paused, "I guess we have another 150 coming, don't we?"

She motioned over to Dan again to grab Stephen's hands. He complied, but the agony of helping Mom was weighing heavy on him. Stephen counted again. This time it was just the strap of the belt.

The "punishment," which is what Mom called this type of event, finally ended. Dan scurried to his room at Mom's release. Mom was not done, though. She ordered Stephen off the couch. The two of them made their way over to the wall with the smudge that had occurred a couple of weeks ago, by Dan's and Stephen's horseplay. Mom did not notice it until this Saturday morning when she came out of her room. Dan was the actual culprit, hitting the chair against the wall and leaving the mark. Nevertheless, he remained quiet about it.

Mom began her 3-hour monologue, at first it was constant yelling which slowly subsided into a conversational tone. She demanded that Stephen's eyes look straight into her eyes. His only choice was to stay in front of her and nod in agreement even though his mind was lost in daydreaming.

This violence continued as her anger kept its energy. Mom slapped Stephen across the face another ten to twelve times. When Stephen's eyes moved from hers, Mom grabbed his chin with her thumb and index finger and squeezed his face upward as she lifted his face to see his eyes again. Spurts of venom from Mom also came in the form of biting his hands and bending his fingers backward until they almost touched the back of his wrist. She would also grab his chin again, but her thumb went inside his mouth as she pressed down below the tongue causing immense pain.

Mom's volume finally lowered, her strength waned, and the violence slowly faded. Her monologue became much more conversational. Everyone was seated. Mom would launch into stories about her dad and her upbringing, or about our dad, or Grandma's travels. Her monologue really could go any which way. Today it was about her days in San Diego and how she met my dad. Her attack on Stephen had started around nine o'clock that morning.

Ann brought me back upstairs. It was four o'clock in the afternoon when we climbed the final stair. She put me on the ground in front of Mom while she went into the kitchen to make dinner. Dan came out of his room, and he took his younger brother outside to play. Mom stretched out on the couch and fell asleep. It was just another day in the life of our home.

I was two years old.

CHAPTER SIX
Resiliency and Strength

"I am reminded of your sincere faith, which first
lived in your grandmother… and, I am persuaded,
now lives in you also."

(II Timothy 1:5 NIV)

"But when the kindness and love of God our Savior
appeared…"

(Titus 3:4 NIV)

C hristmas was almost here. Returning from shopping, the
six of us were singing Christmas carols in that iconic
green Volvo. Volvo's were known for their strength, resistance
to damage, and enduring faithfulness to keep running. It
was embedded in the whole family's memories because of
what it represented.

I am not sure there is a better symbolism to describe
Grandma Lillian, Mom's mom. She came from the District of
Columbia to visit us this Christmas. It was the first time that

I met her. Life was amazing when she was around. She was always warm, and always seemed so authentically interested in who she was listening to. She was like a big, loving teddy bear. As much as she brought kindness, she also brought hope to the landscape of our household. A hope that we cleaved to.

Grandma had experienced much in her life. Mom's dad, her husband, died twenty years before. Her life then was quite different from what it had been with my grandfather. When she helped Grandpa with golf course blueprints and designs, she would do anything to assist. Grandpa often woke up in the middle of the night with a new landscape in mind. Grandma jumped to action, stepping to the drafting board, and drawing what Grandpa envisioned. They had a twenty-six-years age difference, but there was a beautiful harmony between the two until his death.

Grandma and Mom left the Northwest and headed east after Grandpa's death. They settled in Washington, D.C. a short while later. It was where Mom finished high school and where she met her handsome military man. She married Dad shortly before he was deployed, which was for the first two years of their marriage. On military orders, they moved to San Diego, where he was newly stationed. Grandma stayed in D.C. and took on a bookkeeping job for a large, well-known hotel.

We were on Interstate 25 north, driving back from the newly built mall. Grandma was driving and Mom sat in the passenger seat. The four of us children were crowded in the back, with Dan in the middle, Stephen behind Grandma, and Ann behind Mom. I sat on my sister's knee. We were completely out of tune, but the melody of the singing brought an indelible memory. It was so unusual.

Mom reverently feared Grandma. Their relationship was a beautiful mess. The two of them got along quite well, but Grandma had no clue of what was happening within our terror-filled home. Mom was on her best behavior around her mother. The break from the violence and yelling was such a beautiful pause. Grandma's tales also brought a lightness to our very heavy and dark world. Life was rather enjoyable in those moments.

Grandma chugged along the interstate, the highway weaving through the rolling hills that sidled up to the beautiful mountain ranges to the west. The undulating highway was almost a roller coaster as we drove down one side of the hill, bottomed out, and came up the other side.

Letting gravity do its work as we went down the hill, Grandma laughed at how fast she was going. The valley between the hills received the green Volvo. Grandma used the momentum of the downward swing to gain speed on the upswing. Her acceleration met the hill's friction at the full speed limit, and she held it until she reached the top of the climb. Peering over the next hill, everyone gasped loudly, looking up and straight ahead.

My eyes just stared at the obstruction. I sat on Ann's knee and did not make a sound. I took in the large piece of metal across the highway that once was clear. Even for my three-year-old eyes, I recognized that the big trailer was not supposed to be facing that direction. The truck faced the mountains to the west and covered the whole highway. It was the first time I experienced the reality of life's end coming.

What came next was a blur. Without knowing what happened, I was at Ann's feet. Yet, right before she clung to me and swung me behind the passenger seat, I noticed Grandma's hands swiftly turning the car left. A gigantic truck tire enveloped the front of the car. Ann tried to move her body with mine, to subvert any harm, but she went straight into the back of the passenger seat's headrest. Her front tooth went flying from her mouth as the impact swallowed her face. Everything went blank.

I remember the sirens flashing on the ambulance. It was dizzying, relieving our hysteria. Everyone was out of the car and being looked at by professionals. Mom hit her knee hard and received some stitches. Grandma seemed to be fine, but she had two black eyes when she awoke the next morning. Dan was healthy. Stephen's chin ballooned from the jolt against the seat. Ann's face hurt as she was now missing a tooth. Nevertheless, there were no broken bones, and no overnight hospital stays.

Death had come close upon us, but as I have come to realize continuously throughout my life, it had no power. Thanks to some quick wisdom and swift reflexes, the resilience of Grandma Lillian, and the strength of that green Volvo spared us from something much worse. Resiliency and strength were wonderful and remarkable traits that kept us during the horror of ordinary life.

CHAPTER SEVEN

The Plea and The Answer

"Blessed are the peacemakers for they will be called
children of God."

(Matthew 5:9 NIV)

"I love the Lord, for he heard my voice; he heard my
cry for mercy."

(Psalm 116:1 NIV)

Grandma Lila, Dad's mom, instructed us to sit on the
patio as we waited. We were all ready to get home. Still,
we all felt the dread of going home. Mom had just returned
from Washington, D.C. that morning. She had come from
the airport shortly thereafter to pick her four kids up from
Grandma Lila's house.

It had been an unexpected, unconventional, and
worrisome week for us. We learned much more about the
personality under which my dad was brought up. Grandma
Lila was forceful with her rules. However, the structure she

provided was a nice relief from the manic chaos we knew at home.

She loved her gardening and flowers. Beautiful hydrangeas, daffodils, and tulips—along with an azalea bush, junipers, and tomato plants—draped her front yard and were throughout the inside of her home as well. Her house was quaint, without much room for four curious children to meander. The last week wore on all of us, but especially on Grandma Lila.

She had a favorite yellow and green wing chair in the front room of her house. As uncomfortable as that piece of furniture looked, she spent much time sitting in it. From her knitting to her reading, it was her tranquil place. Next to it was a circular end table that was two feet in diameter. Although plants took up much of the space in the room, that circular table held Grandma Lila's sentimental treasure: her King James Bible.

A week earlier, Mom had scurried to the east coast to see her mom, who was recovering from surgery. The hotel where Grandma Lillian worked paid its employees in cash each Friday. Part of her job was to delineate each person's pay into white envelopes and hand out the cash as the shifts ended and the people headed home for the evening.

Darkness was settling into the night sky one evening when a thug with a gun quickly entered the hotel and demanded all the envelopes from Grandma Lillian. It is not clear whether she was completely compliant. Regardless, one bullet resounded from the revolver and hit her. Grandma Lillian fell to the ground, bleeding profusely as he ran out with the money.

When Mom arrived at the hospital, all she knew was that the bullet had gone straight through Grandma Lillian, and she was in surgery. Once Mom heard that her mom was in recovery, she went to her bedside. She remained there until Grandma came out of her induced coma.

Mom paced the room until the doctor arrived, his soft eyes meeting hers as he introduced himself. Checking on Grandma's wounds, he then proceeded to give his report. He confirmed that the bullet had gone straight through Grandma Lillian's body but had not hit any organs. As rotund as Grandma Lillian was, the bullet flew through the right side of her belly and exited through the left side, leaving no serious damage, except that she lost a few pounds.

Mom took a deep breath and looked at her mom in relief. Grandma Lillian chuckled slightly, causing her to ache, but her wit took over. "So, it went through my spare tire?" she quipped. The doctor tried to cover his chuckle and nodded in agreement.

When Mom pulled into the driveway of Grandma Lila's house, she was exhausted. It was obvious that she had not slept well, because one eye drooped much lower than the other. Her insomnia was instantly recognizable as she had displayed it through the years, in accordance with her need to control and abuse. Seeing this, Grandma Lila was taken aback a little as she walked out to the driveway to greet Mom.

Mom feared Dad's mom, even after all the things Grandma Lila had done for her. She was there when Dan had his surgery as a toddler. She was there, defending Mom when Dad left the first time and the second time. And, of course, there was the time she stood up to Dad when he suggested to split the four of us up. In fact, even when Dad left the second time, when he went to visit Grandma Lila along with Jo, his girlfriend, and her two kids, Grandma Lila threw them out of her house and yelled, "Come back when you have your real family with you!" It was the last time she saw her son.

The painful awareness of the tragedies of our family, her grandchildren, gripped her severely. That sagacity came over her when she saw Mom stepping out of the car. She received her well, but Mom was short-tempered and was just trying to get us in the vehicle to leave. Mom's rudeness and Grandma Lila's quiet resistance came to a head. The two stood by the car door for a while, their conversation growing louder, but not enough that any of us sitting on the patio overheard. As a collective, though, we all promptly recognized Mom's agitation and insolence.

We watched as Mom shouted at her mother-in-law. Mom was usually so careful about when she showed her real self. We sat, a little stunned, especially since we knew Grandma Lila's influence over us was powerful. Nevertheless, Grandma stood her ground. She seemed to be pointing out some of the things she had noticed while Mom was away. She spoke of Stephen's bruises, and how she noticed Ann's hair was uneven from chunks of hair being yanked out. Lastly, Grandma confronted Mom on our apparent malnourishment and the toll it had taken on our health and growth.

Mom was not having any of it. She gathered us to get us in the station wagon. She avoided Grandma's eyes until she got in the driver's seat. She looked up at Grandma Lila one last time and pulled out of the driveway. We headed home. Our temporary reprieve from violence and perpetual panic was over.

Grandma Lila watched the car turn at the stop sign until it disappeared. She walked up the driveway, around the pathway of shrubs, bushes, and flowers that gave entrance to the screened-in porch. She could not shake the horror that her family had become. Her head hung low as she grabbed the door handle and walked into that front room. She headed over to her trusted yellow and green chair and sat down. Despair hit her, and tears came slowly and quietly. Pondering what she could have done, or even still could do, to change or influence her family's travails, she muttered to herself an unintelligible prayer.

The room was quiet for fifteen minutes. Her compassion for her grandchildren led to the deepest grief, a grief that Grandma was having a hard time grappling with. She caught her eye on that faithful Bible that lay next to her. The anguish gave way to a light hope. Tears were pouring at this point, and she looked up to the ceiling as if God had suddenly appeared. She spoke earnestly to Him, whom she had come to love and know: "Help! Step in as only You can. Save them!"

An unexpected, yet familiar, still, small voice returned her plea, "Yes!" A pause in His words came as though He was praying and crying with her, "Yes, I will do just that."

CHAPTER EIGHT
Death Came Near

"One look at him and people turned away. We looked down on him, thought he was scum. But the fact is, it was our pains he carried – our disfigurements, all the things wrong with us. We thought he brought it on himself, that God was punishing him for his own failures. But it was our sins that did that to him, that ripped and tore and crushed hm - our sins! He took the punishment, and that made us whole. Through his bruises we get healed. We're all like sheep who've wandered off and gotten lost. We've all done our own thing, gone our own way. And God has piled all our sins, everything we've done wrong, on him, on him!"

(Isaiah 53:3-6 MSG)

No one really knew what set her off.

Mom was vacuuming. She also was cussing under her breath. With no distinguishing pattern with the vacuum, the rug's grain was distorted, with some parts laying down, others standing up. It was hard to tell what was clean and what was not. However, it was clear that Mom's cerebral focus was not on the cleaning.

She called Dan and Stephen into the living room from their bedrooms. She then asked them to explain the discoloration in the rug. Both looked hard at what she was pointing at. Meanwhile, they were freaking out, wondering what would happen if they said the wrong thing. Neither noticed a stain on the rug. Perplexed, they looked at each other, each noticing that the other was shaking.

In a typical moment of torture, Mom would have made both of them—or whomever the accused was—stand at attention. Grabbing the assailed by the chin, and holding it firmly for a couple of minutes, she would demonstrate the power and control that she seemed to enjoy. Then she usually would shake the child's head back and forth viciously, followed by a shouting and spitting lecture on the embarrassment she believed the child had caused her. Lastly, there would be some type of finger bending, her thumb down the child's throat, and/or several slaps across the face. Once her pattern of slogging was finished, she would pull out a belt or other instrument, and the real beating would begin. Today was different.

Dan jumped back suddenly. Stephen flung himself to the ground, screaming and reaching for the left side of his face. The impact of Mom's blows exploded onto the back side of Stephen's left ear. Cradling himself, he pulled his knees all the way to his head. Mom raised the metal vacuum hose up and brought it down hard on his lower ribs. The motion continued for five or six more cycles, hitting the boy from the upper thigh to his shoulder.

Mom reached back to continue the exercise, but Dan lunged at her raging right arm. He blocked and absorbed the impact that was intended for his younger brother. Mom was taken aback by Dan's moment of courage. She warned him. He cowered back into his frail, compliant, and frightful stance. Yet his rage toward her reached a tipping point within in him that he never had experienced before. Nevertheless, he knew there was little he could do to stop the violence.

Mom demanded that Stephen rise. The metal pipe held tightly in her powerful right-handed grip dangled close to the floor. Her temper was not its usual wordiness and defensiveness. She motioned for Stephen to lean into the wall next to the basement door. Everyone in that room knew what was coming next. Her weapon of choice did not change. She told him to strip down to his underwear. He took off his pants and shirt, trembling at her command. The "spanking" began with that very pipe.

The metal ripped at his buttocks. Stephen jumped in place. Once he was still, the metal burned his skin red as she hit the back of his thighs, and his lower back, He jumped up and down, screaming from the pain. Mom warned him about the screeching and threatened him with more if he did not become silent. He bit his tongue as several more swings hit his back side. Stephen could not hold back his tears.

He could no longer stand there and remain calm. My youngest elder brother ran away from the wall. Then she grabbed his arm. He stayed there as she slapped him with the opposite hand. He ran away again, and Mom began chasing him through the living room and kitchen. When she would get close, the pipe met the back of his head, then the side of his head, and finally, smacked him in the face. He fell to the floor, terrified for his life.

Dan was still by the basement door. He was pleading, "Please stop! Please!" The teen's cracking voice was sobbing as he yelled at Mom. She threatened him, telling him to shut up unless he wanted some of the same. Focusing back on Stephen, Mom motioned for him to get up. He lay there bawling and writhing in pain.

She yelled at him three more times, "Get up!" Stephen knew he had no choice but to stand. He did so the best he could, yet he was bent in all the places his body ached or burned. The pipe hit his head several more times. There was no intent to stop.

Dan, fearing for his brother's life, ran toward Mom. She started her forward thrust when Dan caught her on the follow-through. Just before impact on Stephen's head, Dan grabbed the pipe and threw it across the room. Mom was dumbstruck by the gall of her son. She looked straight at Dan. The "angry face" (crunching her forehead's skin, clenching the left side of her teeth, and her lips frowning in an upward, sideways direction) came over her instantly.

Mom turned her attention to Stephen's collar, grabbing and dragging him any which way she desired. They arrived at the basement door. She grabbed the handle and thrust it open so hard that it slammed against the adjacent wall. Dan ran to Mom's side screaming at her as loud as he could. He knew what was next.

Mom hurled Stephen down the eighteen-step staircase. His body tumbled quickly into the darkness. Before the thump of his body landing, the door collided with its frame. Mom locked the door, slapped Dan twice, and walked away.

Heading back to her room, she halted a couple of steps away from the entry. She looked back at Dan and warned him, "If you open that door before morning, you will have the same thing coming to you!" She slammed her bedroom door.

Dan sobbed inconsolably. He did not know if his brother was dead or alive. Then he stopped and listened intently through the door. No audible sound came from downstairs. He crawled up in a fetal position by the lower hinge. He was in absolute terror for his little brother. Wishing he could trade places with Stephen, his hate grew stronger. Exhausted from it all, he fell asleep by the door.

I was four.

CHAPTER NINE
Ode to Joy

"Splendor and majesty are before him; strength and joy are in his dwelling place."

(I Chronicles 16:27)

The family was gathered in the living room when Mom retrieved her Polaroid camera. The instant photo technology was new, and it was quite unusual for us to own anything brand new. Mom was the only one to use it, though. It was part of the gift she received when she earned an incentive award for her outstanding work in her customer service department. I am not sure which she enjoyed more: the camera or the pendant awarded for five years of service. Either way, it was her new toy.

I ran around the center of the room, laughing and giggling. Ann chuckled on the couch against the wall, and Dan watched, leaning on the wall. Stephen laid on his stomach in the middle of the room. Mom sat on the edge of the chair next to the couch, fiddling with the camera.

I climbed on Stephen's back and sat on him. He lost his breath as my weight squeezed his lungs. Gasping for air and chuckling at the same, a noise came out that was entertaining. It tickled me pink. I figured I needed to hear that again, so I lifted my butt up and pounced on his back again. The sound came again, and then again. Cackling took over as I bounced up and down. Stephen motioned for me to stop. Then Mom told me to sit still.

The Polaroid spit out the film. We grabbed the photo from the mouth of the camera and waited for the white of the film to turn into colors, revealing my big laugh. With me still on top of him, Stephen lay on the floor, grinning while his chin rested on his folded arms. A moment now frozen in time, the atmosphere was light and fresh.

Mom put the camera in her oversize bag. This was a day that we did not sit in fear, not for our lives, not for Mom's temper to explode. We did not walk on eggshells, waiting for Mom to erupt because we did something uncalculated or stupid. We knew it could change very quickly, but it was a nice pressure release that we all needed. My childlike innocence brought laughter to all of us. It was one moment that I remember where we really were a family.

We headed out the front door. Mom said the word, and I led the charge out to the car, begging for everyone to hurry, "We must go! We go to the mountains today." The excitement had me grinning from ear to ear. I sat between Dan and Stephen in the back, bouncing up and down on the seat.

Mom took the curves sharply. The mountainside stood straight up on the right while the left side of the car just plunged into an endless valley where the drop over the cliff had no visible end. Then, the road reversed, the mountain was on the left, and the evergreen trees opened into a large valley revealing the mountain ranges on the right. The scene was full of splendor. I loved the grandeur because it freed me from the frozen panic I inadvertently lived out daily. We took another curve as I leaned over Dan's lap. I whispered to myself which was more audible than I realized, "(Sigh)… I love mountains." Mom smiled as she overheard the words.

Mom pulled the car over near the edge of the parking area. It was an overlook, which stood over the Rocky Mountains and all its brilliance. Mom took out the camera from her bag. Ann stood at the edge of the boulders looking down into the hillside valley. Dan and Stephen ran down the trail from the parking area, leaving the rest of us behind. Mom tried to stop them, but she knew her efforts were not working. Instead, she began to take a couple of photos.

I was transfixed. Ann may have been watching me, but I made my own trail to the left side of the parking area. I crouched down and looked at the sight before me. I was a little nervous, but I got within reach of touching a red chipmunk, noticing all its cuteness. My presence did not seem to affect his purpose. He was filling his mouth with nuts from a small bush. I was mesmerized by the storage capacity of his cheeks as they ballooned out.

Ann shouted my name, beckoning me to come to her, or at least to get away from the critter. Mom noticed the commotion. She turned her camera towards me and snapped a photo. Another moment that proclaimed that our family was full of joy. Well, it was, in that moment.

Ann was getting belligerent, calling me to come to her. I was not going to be taken away from what was before me. The chipmunk would have fit in the palm of my hand. I gently reached out to pet his backside. At the sudden appearance of my hand, reaching toward him, he darted away, danced down the hill, and then up the closest tree until he disappeared.

I was standing up, my hand and head pointed straight up. My little finger followed him up the tree. Ann stepped over to my side and clutched my hand that reached for the sky. "Boy, what am going to do with you?" she asked.

Mom called the boys to get back in the car. They complied quickly. Ann sat me down in the car and put me between Dan and Stephen again. Mom plopped down into the driver seat. We drove down the mountainside that we had driven up.

My heart was saddened as the mountain range faded further away, as the car headed back east to go home. Mom told me to get down from the back window. I turned around and sat down, adjusted myself until I got comfortable. My bottom lip slid out. "I want to go back to mountains.," I said. My brothers tried to console me, but my words echoed their feelings.

We drove east on U.S. Highway 36, also known as Boulder Highway, on our way home. Darkness was taking over the daylight as the sun parked itself on the other side of the mountains. The broken clouds in the sky lit up orange across the valley. It was a beautiful sunset, on a perfect day, in what was a fractured and crumbling family.

CHAPTER TEN

Mom's Wife

"Listen to me, O royal daughter; take to heart what I say, Forget your people and your family far away. For your royal husband delights in your beauty; honor him… The bride, a princess, looks glorious in her golden gown. In her beautiful robes, she is led to the king, accompanied by her bridesmaids. What a joyful and enthusiastic procession as they enter the king's palace."

(Psalm 45:10-15 NLT)

Ann finished the laundry and hung it outside to dry on the clothesline. The afternoon was fading into evening, and she still needed to make dinner, pack lunches for the next day, and clean the cat litter as Mom expected. Yet she still had homework that had not even been touched.

Mom depended on her. Ann balanced the checkbook, bought groceries, worked outside in the yard, and took care of her brothers, including cooking for us. What is more, she cleaned the house and took me wherever I needed to be, all the while finding time for school somewhere in between.

The fallout from Mom working so many hours was that all the responsibility fell to the oldest child, Ann. My sister took the role on with diligence, both out of a promise to Dad and the realistic notion that Mom was too narcissistic and jejune to be a good mother. What arose out of her obligations was a confidence of how good she was at it. She was expected to be an adult well before she was ready, called on to raise the boys even though she was far too young for such an ask. This created hostility and competitiveness between her and Dan as well as a distant rapport with Stephen, and an unusually strong bond with me.

Mom had had one of her many migraines earlier in the day. She had lain in her bed all day. When she woke up to get ready for work, it was around 4:30. She disliked working the third shift, but as she would say often, "The things I have to do for this family…" She walked out of her room about 5:30, just as Ann was about to serve dinner. Mom's headache still pounded in her forehead. In obvious discomfort, she was edgy, ornery, and grumpy. The time for her to leave for work was rapidly approaching.

Mom noticed that the cat litter was not clean, plus the bathrooms were needing attention, and I was only half-dressed after my bath. As Dan and Stephen sat at the table, waiting for dinner, Mom started to pull up a seat when she noticed the mashed potatoes were watery. We could feel the tension in the air tightening as we stayed as still as possible, waiting for Mom to leave for work. Typically, it was a respite when she left, even though we usually went to bed shortly thereafter, thanks to Ann's tight scheduling.

It seemed Mom was about to take her seat at the table. Instead, she picked up the pan of potatoes, walked with her heels pounding the floor, and threw the pan into the sink. Ann was cutting my meat when she heard the clanging from the sink. Almost crying, she knew she could not show it. She stood straight up at the same moment Mom met her at the table.

Mom laid into her daughter loudly and vehemently: "Can't I ask one thing of you, or do I have to do all the workaround here?" Ann boiled inside at the audacious statement. Grabbing Ann's lengthy, blonde hair, Mom pulled until Ann's head bent backward. Ann winced.

Mom pushed Ann across the room until she fell on her back end. She stomped across the floor again, meeting the teenager at her landing spot. Mom pulled Ann's hair tightly until Ann was on her feet, looking Mom eye to eye. I watched from the dinner table barely able to contain the scream that threatened to escape.

Mom spent the next hour berating Ann for the work that was not done around the house, blaming her for dinner not being ready, and suggesting that Ann was making her late for work. Ann could only agree with Mom's perception of reality, that she was responsible for everything that went wrong.

Mom headed towards the couch and fell to a sitting position. Her migraine was excruciating now. Putting her head against the back of the couch, she tried to relieve the pressure. She was already late for work, so she picked up the telephone and, speaking in a sickly monotone, informed her boss that she would not be at work. She was home for the night, but the night had only begun.

Mom discontinued trying to find things that were not finished or were undone; instead, she shifted to Ann herself. One of the special moments of each week was when Ann attended Job's Daughters at a local church. It was the only thing that she ever asked Mom to allow her to do outside of the house. Otherwise, her full attention was on the house, her brothers, her schoolwork, and, mostly Mom. She considered herself Mom's wife.

Ann's room was her sanctuary, her resting place, her solace, and the place where she expressed her loves, beliefs, and dreams. She hung posters all over the walls. There were several sentimental things throughout her special place, including Jesus signs that hung from the ceiling. Ann was blossoming and beginning to find what she loved in life, even in an extremely limited capacity. She had few friends, but the ones she had were special.

When Mom turned her ferocity towards Ann, it was more than intruding on her space; it tore at her soul. Mom walked into Ann's room. Shoving all that was on the dresser onto the floor, she broke a piece of pottery and cracked a picture frame. Mom then opened all the drawers, flinging Ann's clothes across the room and ripping up the ones that disgusted her.

Pulling all the bedclothes off the bed, she stood on the bed's surface, snatching down the stringed-up signs and hurling them to the floor. Stepping off the bed, Mom tore every poster and picture that was on the wall. To Ann's horror, every special thing that she owned was tossed across the room. Her resentment and animosity toward Mom were setting in. Mom broke everything in that room, including Ann's heart.

Dinner was forgotten and there was no asking about it (that would have bad consequences). We boys went to bed. Dan and Stephen tucked me in, and they headed to their bedroom downstairs. It was just Mom and Ann now. Mom spent the next three hours bashing her firstborn verbally, along with moments of holding Ann's chin until it reddened and bruised. Pulling back Ann's fingers and yanking her hair were constant through it all.

I could hear Ann's cries and Mom's shouting until I dropped off to sleep. It created a frozen dread within me, part of the perpetual state of terror in our home. There was no wrong that could be undone, no life lived, nor friendship maintained. Instead, life centered around Mom, her control, her manipulation, and the cruelty she enforced.

The threats, destruction, violence, and barrage of verbal abuse and hatred stopped about 11:30. Mom left Ann to herself inside her room, closing the door behind her as she left. Ann sat on the floor, her palms on her forehead, and wept.

Mom went to the kitchen, grabbed the Wonder Bread in the cupboard, pulled two pieces out, and ate them. Snatching the Excedrin, she pulled out four pills and swallowed each whole, without water. She went to the living room, stretched out on the couch, rolled over so that she was facing the cushions, blotting out any light. Her stillness gave way to sleep.

Ann spent the rest of the night cleaning her room, sobbing through most of it. Sleep was not an option and hatred replaced any notion of obligation that she so compulsively fulfilled. That night brought the initiation of her plan to leave our home as soon as she could.

I was six.

CHAPTER ELEVEN

Everything Changed

"The Lord your God in your midst, The Mighty One,
will save; He will rejoice over you with gladness, He
will quiet you with His love, he will rejoice over you
with singing."

(Zephaniah 3:17 NKJV)

Mom was on her hands and knees, picking each tile up off the floor. The adhesive, which normally sealed the tiles down, apparently was gone. Mom picked up each tile separately as though she had just bought them from the flooring store. She was aghast and bound to find out what happened. She would pursue it not in an investigative way, but rather, by way of accusation, confession, and force.

Mom had gotten home from work a short time before this. She had gone to get water in the kitchen when she tripped over a loose tile. It did not take her long to assume who was at fault and to make her accusation. Going down to the basement, where Stephen was in his room, she grabbed him by the hair, waking him from a deep sleep, and pulled him all the way upstairs. She did not let go until the light was shining down on the kitchen floor, exposing the bare cement.

All Stephen could do was watch as Mom pulled the flooring up. He was lost for words, and clueless about how the tiles came undone. Mom was all over the kitchen, realizing the whole floor was loose. It was a horrible day.

She became unbelievably violent. All the normal things went on: the bending back of his fingers, her hand on his jaw, her finger in his mouth, her sitting on him with all her weight until he was wheezing and his back was bent over the railing. Those were common and normal. This time, the unusual flared up as well.

The belt with the buckle hit every part of Stephen, from neck to ankle. The metal vacuum pipe came back out, and the endless, creative ways to beat him did not stop. It was a horrible day. It was an unbelievably long day, leaving Stephen bruised, broken, and barely able to stand or walk.

All of us were horrified and terrified. Mom had never gone this far before. I hid in my room as did Ann and Dan. When Mom finally stopped, she was visibly exhausted. She went to her room for the rest of the day.

Stephen stayed home from school because there was no way to hide those contusions and welts from the nursing staff, teachers, and principal. After the brutality lasted through the night and kept us awake, the rest of us went to school as if it were any normal morning. Stephen lay in bed ailing and crying in disbelief.

Sometime later, Mom called Grandma Lillian. They had been talking for a long time. She explained how Stephen had "pried each tile up." And then asked rhetorically, "Why would he do such a thing?" She went on, bringing up the way she was "left holding the bag" after Dad left. She detailed how she had to discipline Stephen by using the belt and that it left a couple of bruises.

Her denial, deflections, and defense continued: "My intentions were good. I never meant to do anything to hurt anyone. I would never dare to do that… I do not bear grudges; that's just not me. I was not raised that way… I don't mean to be personal about all of this, but I've got two sides to me… I'm getting down to the nitty-gritty, and I don't normally talk like this, but you know I don't complain. It isn't easy taking care of everything… I've got enough headaches right now. I have all I can handle."

Grandma Lillian listened intently, compassionately, and knew it was time for her to step in. Mom knew that Grandma needed to act also. (I will not go so far as to say that she knew that she would kill Stephen, but there was a conscious acknowledgment that she had gone too far.) Apparently, the realization of her actions set in deeply, although she would never admit or confess such a thought, nevertheless, she seemed scared of what she might do next.

A short while later, Stephen was on a Trailways bus heading east, from Denver to Washington, D.C. Mom sent my twelve-year-old brother on a bus heading east by himself. It was unfathomable considering Mom barely let any of us out of her sight or control. She was desperate, though, and desperate times require desperate measures. Things were clearly shifting, and none of us knew how to react to it all.

He arrived and Grandma Lillian met him at the airport. He was astonished by his new surroundings. He had waited for this day of getting away from Mom for seven years, and now here he was. Grandma drove the two of them home. He found his new room, in a foreign place. He attended his new school, where he had no friends and no familiarity. However, he was free.

He had arrived at Grandma Lillian's on his thirteenth birthday. Jealousy and sadness sunk in as I mourned my brother's leaving. Part of me wanted to be on that bus in place of him, or at least beside him. What really hurt was that my closest friend was gone.

It later came to Mom's attention that, a few days before she discovered the tiles were loose, the kitchen sink had overflowed, dissolving the adhesive that held the tile to the cement floor. As was the case in most situations, Mom never expressed regret for her destructive reactions.

Yet something broke in her. The physical abuse did not stop, but it slowed. The self-absorption and control were still constant. Nevertheless, her assault-and-attack-first tactic transformed into defense, denial, and deflection at all costs. Something broke in Mom that day in such a way that no remorse was noticeable, yet everything changed.

The atmosphere was still very charged, frenetic with fear. Her intolerance to failure was unwavering, but something changed in all of us. Ann was ready to leave. Dan was learning new courage and strength to go along with his growing hatred. Stephen, for the first time, was separated from the constant daily abuse.

Something changed in me also. The constant state of panic for the first six years of my life was over, but so was the protection that kept me from harm. A new form of terror was beginning to settle in, and it was worse than anything I understood or underwent until now. A realization of how alone I had always been was beginning to settle deep within me.

The emotional and mental separation of my siblings commenced with Stephen's departure. It was the first sign that our family unit was dismantling and crumbling. It had started with Dad's explosive desertion and betrayal and then continued with Mom's war-zone style focus on minutiae for the last six years. Now the cracks in our family's foundation deepened with the tide of separation.

I felt overwhelmed by this new isolation, lost in a world I did not know. I was unable to recognize, receive, or give love in any way. I was overcome with trembling far more than I ever had felt before. Being at war and trying to survive it—well, that was all I knew.

I was a week away from my seventh birthday.

CHAPTER TWELVE
Alone and Afraid

"He existed before anything else, and he holds all creation together."

> (Colossians 1:17 NLT)

"He has mercy upon whomever he wills, and he hardens the heart of whomever he wills."

> (Romans 9:18 RSV)

"His love endures forever."

> (Psalm 136)

I t was a cold, snowy morning in October. These types of storms came through often during the middle of autumn. Mom was prepping and coaching me as she got me ready for school. Her tone was calm, reflective, and a little unnerving: "If anyone asks, tell them that you hit your chin against the door." I nodded my head in agreement. It had been a long day already. My face hurt from the manhandling of my jaw, my tongue, my fingers, and from each slap she landed across my cheeks.

Mom came downstairs the day before. I was playing in the basement. She was set off by something she saw, and suddenly, she turned and focused her rage towards me, slapping and throwing her youngest son. As she came back upstairs with me in tow, she then said, "Boys (talking to Dan and Stephen), get to school. Dale is staying home from school today." My brothers were terrified for my safety. They left and I was alone with my tormentor. All I recall is the isolating and deathly terror I was under.

Stephen talked Dan into visiting the administration office to tell them how afraid they were of what she might do. They talked to a counselor. It was the first time anyone was informed of our family's horrific home-life. However, no one was questioned or investigated.

Mom applied four bandages this morning. Two of them were circular as she placed them on the bruised spots where her thumb and index fingers pressed into my jaw. One rectangular, elastic dressing was placed under my chin where her index finger held my head in place while she pressed down her thumb under my tongue. The last circular bandage was placed in front of my left ear where the tip of her middle finger welted my cheek. She gave me a kiss on the forehead and sent me off. I ran through the snow, trying to get to school on time.

At school, I faced a confusing and overwhelming confrontation each day. I missed my brother walking to school with me. It was not that long ago that we had attended the same school. Then, he had gone east. When Stephen had been shipped out, I became deathly afraid of where Mom's wrath would shift or on whom it would be taken out. My terror rose. I felt as if Stephen had been stolen from me. My bitterness also rose.

As a matter of fact, after his departure, everything had turned on its head. Although the tortuous nature of things before was horrendous and terrifying, there was a familiarity to it all. Plus, everyone saw to it that I was hidden or protected from the danger most of the time. If I was not with Ila, our caretaker who was also a refuge for me, then Ann had taken care of me. If Ann could not, Dan had watched out for me, even though we really were never close. Then there was Stephen; he just took a liking to me. Even Mom previously had made sure that I was not around when awful things happened. In any case, things changed, and the familiarity was gone now that Stephen was back.

He had returned from Grandma Lillian's not too long ago, but things were quite different. Upon his return, Mom's violent rage lessened. Still, it was not completely halted.

Things did not return to the status quo, where violence was normal, and I was insulated or buffered from it. For the first time, surviving relied on me, so I began to cocoon myself from all perceived threats and terrors. This is also the moment that I learned to loathe the boy that I could never let anyone see—the real me. This paradox of survival and hatred warred within me. One fought to protect and shelter Dale at any cost. The other sought to dismantle and destroy Dale.

From here on, Mom's rage and physical abuse only showed themselves in weekly moments, whereas before it occurred three or four times a week on average. Dan was the culprit for many of the things Mom poured her rage out on, and he was a master at letting the "discipline" fall on his brother or sister. Regardless, Mom was demonic in her wrath.

Stephen was now in junior high school. However, not only was he at a different school, but he also was not the same brother. After he arrived back home four months after being shipped out east, Stephen's countenance brightened. Before he left, my brother was lost and aimless. When he returned, he was poised with a certainty never seen before. This change in his self-confidence emanated from the affection he received from Grandma, and it lingered well past their time together. Stephen now had an outlet where he could go if the violence started again.

In contrast, loneliness set in me intensely. I felt naked in a reality that I could not pretend did not exist any longer. Yet the most terrifying part was about to come. Stephen was maturing, Dan was distant, and Ann was around less and less. Mom was the one person who stayed. Up to that point, I had spent my life darting and dashing from her. Now, she was the one person I could not avoid. She was still very frightening to be around, especially with the realism that she had no ability or intention to care about or for any of us.

Mom's physical assaults diminished greatly after Stephen came home. However, in its place rose a new, consuming terror for me: my soul was engulfed by her selfish vanity. This new existence was lived out in obedience to her demands. I was in a state of constant and frozen dread necessitated because rage would rise at any given moment. If rage was not present, then the obsessive panic set in keeping all things quiet and contained as to not disturb her. Her physical attacks came in a less abusive style, but they still came. And I was in complete and utter isolation, inside our home and outside.

I made it through the first couple of hours of that school day, daydreaming and gazing at the snow outside. Recess passed with me playing in the sandbox by myself. I tried to have friends, but I had no idea how to be one. In my attempt to play with others, I would steal the ball or bury their toys in the sand. When I played games, I was highly competitive, setting out to win no matter the cost. I just wanted to fit in. However, I quickly learned that I did not. I was short in stature and puny in strength. My comfort came when I was playing or sitting by myself.

Gym was the next item on the school agenda. The game that day was kickball. Before we even began, we had to change into our gym clothes in the locker room, where my garments were stolen from my locker and hidden. My underwear almost became my new hat as some mischievous boys yanked it upwards. Once the teacher intervened, I came out and joined the other students. Teams were chosen, and as usual, I stood until the last person was picked.

Our team was up. A big kid took the rolling ball across home plate and booted it out to center field. He stood on second when the girl I had a crush on came to the plate. The ball rolled to her and she pushed the ball towards third base. She ran as hard as she could and reached first, and I screamed loudly. The big guy was out at third. A tall, frail boy headed to the plate before me and kicked the ball to second, where the fielder mishandled the ball. They stood on first and second when I came to the plate.

A thought swam through my head: "What if I miss… again?" I was petrified, standing in the home plate box, but I was also excited. The ball rolled towards me, my foot caught the ball flush across the shoelaces and the ball went flying.

I stood in amazement for a second before I heard, "RUN!" My short legs ran around first until I reached second safely. My pretend girlfriend and the frail boy crossed the plate, and my teammates jumped up and down in excitement. I was stunned.

We returned to the classroom. The teacher began her lesson when a message came in from the nurse's office. I was asked to come to the front. The vice-principal (VP) came and escorted me to the nurse. When we arrived, the nurse and VP asked me many questions. They asked for me to undress, stand, and turn around. They seemed satisfied enough when I put my clothes back on.

The nurse took off my bandages. Her tone was gentle, but I was freaking out. In no way could they find out about my home. There was one terrifying thought that came over and over, "What if Mom knew I told…?" I intended to be as silent as I could. The questions came in many different patterns, but my resolute response was exactly what Mom commanded me, "I ran into my door at home." I spent the rest of the day in the vice-principal's office until the last bell rang. Nothing came of their interrogation and investigation. Released from their presence, I ran the whole way home!

Not one of my siblings was there when I arrived. Mom was sleeping. I went to my room, found a few sturdy pencils, and we—the announcer, narrator, and referee, in the form of three pencils—had our first boxing match of the day. A few of the contenders broke in half, but the tension eased as I announced, narrated, and refereed the pencil bouts on the floor.

Mom stepped out of her room and went to the kitchen. She poured cold coffee into a pan and heated it on the stove. Ann got home after spending time with friends. She darted straight into her room. When Dan and Stephen arrived from school, they went out and played, at Mom's urging. I peeked out of my room to see my family, but they all had dispersed by the time I was in the living room. Sadness came over me, and aloneness was my new shelter and miserable friend. I went back to narrating the greatest pencil fight in history.

The damage from Mom's physical torture destroyed our home well after Dad's explosive exodus, which had left us in ruins years before. A new normal was now in place. Without comprehending it, with Mom's abuse and Dad's absence, I was dangerously alone. My life was already devastated with their desertion, abandonment, and neglect. When Mom withheld nurture, and Dad's heart discarded his son, a loathsome terror set in. It maliciously pounded me into submission, and a new belief system took shape: I was worthless, and no one could convince me otherwise. What was to come next cemented my belief that I was a horrible mistake, a weapon of choice, and an unwanted mess.

I was seven.

CHAPTER THIRTEEN

Shattered

"I Am God Almighty (El-Shaddai, "The All Sufficient One," or "The God of the Mountain"); Walk [habitually] in Me [with integrity, knowing that you are always in My presence]..."

(Genesis 17:1 AMP)

Ann stared back at Mom, immobilized by fear. Yet her contempt for Mom had given her courage, purpose, and determination. Her eyes were steadily fixed on Mom's next move. Mom, her fists clenched and her "angry face" grimacing, was fixated on Ann. I stood cowardly behind Mom, next to the upstairs bedroom, watching.

Dave was here to take Ann away. She had been seeing him for a good while, and it was the first time I had seen his charming grin and striking black hair. He was handsome.

Ann was eighteen at the time. Before this moment, she had discussed her situation with many of her friends, her pastor at the local church we attended very irregularly, and a few other people. Their counsel was not universal, except in one thing: Ann needed to get away from Mom. Ann had wrestled with herself as she struggled to reach this decision, knowing the effect it would have on her brothers. Ultimately, the counsel she received solidified her decision. She had served, slaved over, and given everything to Mom. Now, for the first time, she said aloud, "It is time for me to go!"

Dave's presence ignited Mom in a way I had rarely witnessed before. She exploded, shouting and stomping until she stood in front of Ann. Her daughter quaked and shrieked. She took a couple of steps backward at Mom's advance. Mom grabbed Ann's long, gorgeous hair and pulled until her head snapped back as if she were about to have whiplash. Ann screamed. Mom let go only to find blond hair in her clasped fist. I was shaking in the corner, observing.

Mom's continuous yelling and Ann's nodding or quiet answering had gone on for a couple of hours at this point. Although Dave had been in the house, he now walked back outside to his car, realizing that his presence was not helping. As he left, he whispered to Ann, asking her to finish what she committed to do, what he came to do.

Mom released Ann's hair and pushed her full force into the railing next to the stairs that led to the front door. I ran across the living room as fast as my feet would go, wanting to get between Ann and Mom. However, panic stopped me in my tracks as I reached the wall beside the staircase.

Ann cleverly escaped the entrapment Mom had intended at the railing. Startled by the nerve and craftiness of her daughter, Mom chased Ann around the room. Her expletives were constant, as were Mom's endless comparisons of Ann to Dad. The hatred Mom unleashed in Ann was at an almost lethal level.

Mom and Ann came to a complete stop in front of the steps, with Ann pleading with Mom, "Please end this charade." Ann continued, saying the words she had been longing to say all day, "Mom, I have to go. I must go! You know I do. I have…" Before Ann could finish, Mom's hand met Ann's cheek and swiveled her head. As I witnessed it all, my heart was breaking.

Ann darted down the stairs, turned, and looked back up, where our eyes met. I started bawling. Mom stepped away for a minute and returned with a dining room chair held high above her head. I ran and stepped in front of Mom, having no idea what I was doing. Suddenly, my scream cried out Mom's name, and shrieked, "NO!" It felt as if my entire insides came out of my body with that scream. Apparently, Mom did not notice.

Instead, she screamed profanities in a rant mixed with Ann's name. She flung the chair like a baseball, throwing it over her right shoulder and down the stairs, directly in Ann's path. My sister saw the chair hurtling at her as she turned toward the door and grabbed the handle. Daylight illuminated the stairwell. Then the chair somersaulted three times and smashed into Ann's face, and the impact slammed her to the floor. She rose to her feet and slithered through the door holding her nose in obvious pain. The blood dripped from her chin and her hand.

I ran after her, wailing uncontrollably. Ann was already by the car with Dave next to her. Dan and Stephen had been told to go outside earlier. Their quiet reaction was as if they knew this was coming. I yelled, "Ann, please don't go!" and fell to my knees.

She looked back and we caught each other's glance again. Ann mouthed the words, "I'm sorry," then gazed my way for a few seconds more. Turning, she let go of Dave's hand and headed for the passenger-side door without looking back. The car started, accelerated, and disappeared. I shivered, not from the cold, but from the cavernous hole that I felt. My real, unnatural mom was gone. Meanwhile, Mom stayed inside and went to her bedroom. She was not seen for the rest of the day.

I was eight years old.

CHAPTER FOURTEEN

The Man Who Wrestles, The God Who Calls

"Once more I will astound these people with wonder upon wonder."

(Isaiah 28:14 NIV)

Stephen stood to his feet, three feet in front of me. Kicking the coffee table aside, he suddenly became very lively. I could not tell if his jerky hand motions, foot-tapping, raised voice, and persistent, animated monologue was a sign that he was frustrated with me. Perhaps he was just extremely intense due to his recent encounter with Mom. Maybe he was expressing excitement that he could not contain. "Maybe it was all of the above," I thought to myself.

I was irritated with him at this point, ready to run out of the room. In reaction to his movements, emotions were flooding me, and anxiety made me jumpy. I felt as if I were about to act, but I do not know what I was going to do. If this had been like most of the unsettling moments at home, I would have been cringing with angst or disgust, ready to bolt for the door. To my surprise, I stayed.

The previous night had been painfully lonely. Mom let Stephen leave with his friend. It still baffles me. It was the first time I was alone in the house. It also was the first time that Mom had let Stephen leave for any reason other than when he had gone to stay with Grandma Lillian. One of Dan's acquaintances, who was more friendly toward Stephen, had invited my younger brother to his house for an overnight stay.

There was no better way to notice Mom's recent change than in her response to Stephen. Whether it was her realization that she could not control everything or her exhaustion from all the previous wars, Mom let him go! For whatever reason, Mom was relinquishing her firm grip on her kids. It is not like Stephen ever asked for anything. As a matter of fact, this was the first time he had asked for anything outside the home.

Dan still lived at home, but he was not around much. He was either with friends or in his room. Ann had not returned. So, I was alone, not sleeping much. In my insomnia, I reasoned that this is how our dog, Andy, felt when Dan's friends would throw firecrackers at his feet. He hissed and howled at the fright as he jumped from here to there trying to avoid being hit by the combustion of the loud popping noises. Ultimately, he would run to his doghouse in horrific fright and his tail cowered between his legs. Similarly, the loneliness was setting in, and the fear of it all made me curl up until I held my knees to my chest.

Mom had gone to work this morning, but it was one of her last days. She had shifted from her nightshift to days a couple of years back. Everyone in our house was now preparing for our big move to the east coast. Mom had put in her paperwork to transfer a few days earlier.

Stephen had returned home around mid-morning. It was hard to tell if he had even slept, but the bags under his eyes told the story. Yet I had never seen him even close to this level of excitement. His energy was vibrant. The change in him was palpable and contagious.

I sat there listening to his story, mesmerized. Stephen's thoughts unfolded in front of me, "We were up all night! We laughed, wrestled, and engaged in conversation all night. I haven't slept at all." There was a release in the air with his words, an unusual light-heartedness about him. I sat there in amazement as he talked about the fun he had.

He noticed my intrigue. He went on to describe the conversation, but I did not comprehend completely what he was talking about. I could only wish I had been with him in the scene he described in detail. Jealousy began rising, and anger floated to the surface. I felt as if I had been left behind.

After all, I intimately knew that sentiment. I continued to listen, though, captivated by the freedom of his words.

Stephen continued, "We went to his house at first. We settled a few miles away next to a pond near some tennis courts where my friend and I had played tennis after staying up all night. (His dad drove us there at like 6 am in the back of his pickup truck.) I wanted the peaceful calm my friend exhibited. Then, he asked me to pray, and, well, I could only follow his lead. We had our eyes closed, and, after wrestling with God and finally giving Him my life, we opened our eyes to the sun coming up right over the pond," he paused being caught up in the story.

It was clear that he was changed by the moment he was describing. He continued his lavish details: they laid down on the ground taking in the view in front of them. He was given a front-row seat to the rise and fall of the mountains and valleys of the Rockies. The sun had risen from the east, lighting up the low hanging clouds in a lovely auburn shade. They dripped their colors as they draped over the majesty of the mountains to the west. Stephen's excitement filled the room as he wrapped up, "The pond perfectly reflected the sun, which was huge, red, and orange. Then, about a million blackbirds swooped down in front of us. My mouth hung open. I was amazed by God's personal and intimate love. It was like God made the day just for me!" His expression said everything that his words portrayed.

Liberty and tranquility filled my senses. I sat on that hillside with Stephen and his friend, if only in my imagination. I was lost in a wonderful playland when I noticed Stephen's lips were still moving. Reality came over me. Then incessant rage filled me. I started to despise this conversation and I reasoned myself into despair.

"How can you ever think such a place exists, and even if it did, that it's really for you!?" I asked venomously, my hate coming out. I jumped up from the sofa as my rage took over. "Don't play me!" I shouted. Stephen looked like he was in shock. However, it did not stop his persistence.

He raised his voice to match mine and repeated something he had said earlier: "You've got to do this, Dale! It's the only way, the only possible way out!"

I looked at him, my feet dancing circles around the room. I was freaking out. My heartbeat pounded, causing my chest to vibrate. Stephen sat down and beckoned me to come, patting the cushion next to him.

"I can't! I CAN'T!" I said. My feet kept spinning around the room until I collapsed. Putting my hands over my ears, I rose to my knees. I wanted to run to my room, but I could only muster enough energy to remain on my knees, collapsing my head and arms onto the sofa cushion.

My brother's tone softened immensely, "I know you're scared."

I looked up at the iconic, golden sundial clock that had hung on the wall ever since I was born. The morning was gone. We had been at this for four hours. Incensed that Stephen had stolen my time, I finally relented, got up from my knees, and sat next to my brother.

The reason he had taken all this time to extend his invitation to pray became clear. I shifted in my seat, becoming fidgety from the trust I tried to arouse. I nodded in agreement that I was willing.

At Stephen's suggestion, I repeated his words. They were short and we were done. I wondered what I was supposed to feel. I considered my brother's story, as he had told it over the last few hours.

When he had talked about his conversion from the night before, the emotions were obvious and conclusive. There was freedom as if handcuffs had been undone. My brother had experienced a breakthrough as if the bars he had been behind had been broken now. Confidence and belief came from him that I had never seen. Then, there was the fun, the camaraderie, and the wonder of the night before. His experience was filled with a dazzling array of sensations, and a newness emoted from Stephen.

I felt nothing. I was worried that I had done something wrong. I tried to ask Stephen about it, but he had already left the room. My eyes caught the hands of the clock again as I took in the time. I sat on that couch with no sensation, but what did come was startling. My jitters waned. My panic was calmed. My anger and hatred released.

The room was light and serene. A Presence, one that I cannot explain, sat with me. His eyes watched and winked. Peace emanated from Him and sweetly entered my soul.

I turned ten years old biologically; however, my inner man, my spirit, was born… again.

CHAPTER FIFTEEN

The Journey Between the End and the New

"'But don't you have just one blessing for me, Father? Oh, bless me my father! Bless me!' Esau sobbed inconsolably."

(Genesis 27:38 MSG)

"Wake up, you sleepyhead city! Wake you, you sleepyhead people! King-Glory is ready to enter. Who is this King-Glory? God-of-the-Angel-Armies: he is King-Glory."

(Psalm 24:9-10 MSG)

I could only think about the last moment I had seen Dan before we left. He had looked content, yet he was lost. Strong, seemingly confident, and looking to the future in his newfound freedom on his own, he still was searching for who he was. I grinned, a bit in awe, especially as he showed off his muscles. After all, I was a puny and scrawny kid. What was most memorable was his eyes as he looked back over his right shoulder, smiling as he waved with the back of his hand. Those blue eyes stayed with me the whole trip.

The Ford Pinto wagon was jam-packed. There was no visible space to be seen from the back of the headrests to the hatchback handle. With the exhaust pipe hanging two inches off the ground, the vehicle looked as if it were an arrow about to be shot upwards from its bow.

Mom took the driver's seat as Stephen waited for me to get in the middle. I crawled into the makeshift seat, which was more of an armrest, while Stephen got in and buckled up. With my shoulders squished between the armpits of my traveling compadres, my eyes barely saw the road ahead. The five-day road trip was underway.

We had spent much of the day before packing. Mom delivered the items we were not taking with us to other people. She had sold some of it, but a leased storage unit in Denver would house most of the things she owned. Whatever was left was stuffed into the back of that Pinto. Dan had helped to pack and move many of the items—that is until he and Mom had it out.

As Dan had aged through his high school years, he and Mom had grown apart. Her fondness for and protection of her eldest son waned, especially the more he exerted his independence and shunned the family. He stepped away from the house often, even more so after he graduated, drinking and partying a lot. When he was home, he locked himself in his room. His rage would come to life when Mom tried to gain access to his private abode by pounding on the door. In his room, Dan felt liberated from Mom's physical dominance, but she still had great command of his heart. Plus, Mom applied a narcotic monologue that got all of us to bend to her will and influence.

Today had already been a long day. Dan had gotten home from work around 3 p.m. that afternoon and immediately began moving boxes, furniture, and more. I did my part, but it was Dan and Stephen who got things where they needed to be. We were all tired, especially Mom. I am not sure what happened outside when they were trying to pack the trailer for the storage unit, but Mom was irked by what she perceived as careless handling of her things. She gave Dan a dirty look and then decided to confront him once they reached the doorway to the house.

They both walked up the flight of stairs, the same steps where Mom had hurled the dining chair at Ann a couple of years before. Once Mom reached the top step, she turned around and slapped Dan. He stood a head taller than Mom in his full adult-sized body now. His arms were larger than Stephen's and mine put together. So, Mom was frail against his strength, although she stood there, giving him some good wallops.

The methods she used to use just were not penetrating past Dan's girth. Unlike the rest of us, Mom rarely manipulated his fingers to bend them back, nor would she hold his jaw so that it could be moved at her whim. Instead, desperate to show control, she grabbed his biceps and squeezed. Dan took a couple of slaps across the face, but his anger flared up and his eyes said, "Enough." It was not going to continue much longer.

Moving around that living room, shifting from offensive to defensive positions, Mom let go of Dan's biceps as he flexed, trying to show his physical prowess. Mom's yelling and degrading of her son continued perpetually. On this particular guilt trip, she mentioned his slowness, how she was the only one there for him, and how Dad wanted nothing to do with him.

Dan countered with his own history of events. My eyes were wide open as he laid open the reality of what happened to Stephen and Ann a short time ago. He contradicted Mom's remembrance of when Dad was around. Up until this time, no one dared to go where Dan invaded.

His temper was at full tilt, matching Mom's shouting level, word for word, tit for tat. It was my first witness of Mom's denial, defiance, and deflection of anything that had happened just a few years before. Mom's only response indicating that she recalled any of the physical violence was to say, "Stephen deserved everything he got." This outraged Dan so much that his veins popped out of his skin.

Mom's aggression escalated, and words were no longer needed. She opened her mouth, baring her teeth. Then she turned her neck, thrust her head forward, and attempted to bite Dan's nose. He moved just in time, catching her cheek with his head as he turned to the side and back. Grabbing Dan's arms, Mom shoved him against the wall. He stumbled back a step, the wall prevented him from falling.

Gaining his composure and balance, he grabbed her arms firmly until she could not move them. He hated violence passionately and thought it wrong to assault her, so he let go. Upon the removal of his grip, Mom swung her right arm, slapping him flush in the face. Dan raised his arm in the same way when he slapped her back. Mom went staggering back a couple of steps. She incited Dan even more by saying, "Well, I can see that you are just like your father." This was a strange comparison considering Dad did not raise his hand against Mom when they were together.

She grabbed the belt to whack Dan with the buckle, but before Mom could get a handle on the leather, Dan ripped the belt from her hands. It was interesting to see Mom befuddled at Dan's physical strength. However, for her, physicality was not her only weapon. Her tongue could usually turn any situation to her advantage. In this case, though, she did not know how to handle Dan's tactical measures to stop her. She attempted again by grabbing his arms and pushing, but he stood his ground and flexed. Then, he intentionally grabbed her biceps and heaved her across the living room.

She went flying, briefly landing on her back heel. Trying to catch her balance, she kept putting her feet down, one after the other, but the momentum was too much. Her backside smashed into the wall and gravity pulled her to the floor. Her loss of breath and shriek of pain was staggering to watch. Dan flew down the steps and out the door. The vibrations shook the house.

Mom slowly got up. She walked gingerly to her room and shut her door, wincing as she went. I hated what I saw, but Dan became somewhat of a hero to me in that moment. It made me mad that anyone would do that to Mom, but the audacity of his standing up to her impressed me.

Later, as I woke up from my slumber between Mom and Stephen, Dan's eyes still penetrated my consciousness. I had lost another family member that day. It was not as painful as when Stephen was sent away, or when my sister left with Dave, whom she ended up marrying. I was not as close to Dan as to the other two. Still, this moment left me feeling alone again, although, the sting of it was soothed by having Stephen right next to me.

Mom navigated Interstate 70 in an unconventional driving style. If someone was too close, she stared out the rearview mirror while cussing them out. She hated and feared truckers, trying to avoid them. The lane lines seemed to be only a suggested boundary at times. But we drove, and drove, and drove…

Five days later, my crunched-up bones wiggled out of the car. There was Grandma Lillian, her infectious smile, and her "spare tire." I wrapped my arms as far as I could around her body and squeezed. We had arrived at our new home, a two-bedroom apartment for the four of us. It overlooked Iwo Jima National Park, the Potomac River, and the Washington, D.C. Mall. At the edge of Arlington, Virginia, overlooking our nation's capital, a new life awaited.

I was still ten.

CHAPTER SIXTEEN
The Cover-Up

"But made himself of no reputation, and took upon the form of a servant, and was made in the likeness of men."

(Philippians 2:7 KJV)

"A father to the fatherless… Is God in His Holy Habitation."

(Psalm 68:5 AMP)

Grandma Lillian was fixing dinner, and the smells from the kitchen were intoxicating, unlike anything I had experienced when Colorado was our home. I sat on the long, arching couch against the wall in our thousand square-foot apartment, the aromas and sizzling sounds drawing me into the kitchen. I asked Grandma, "What you makin'?" Peering over her shoulder, she smiled but did not answer. I gave up my inquisition and went back to the couch, pulling on the on-button on the 20" tubed-television.

I watched TV, having arrived back at the apartment from my typical seventh-grade school day. Although school was not extremely hard, I had not made any friends. In fact, friendship was a foreign word to me, so it surely did not seem to be an option. Since others had made all my decisions for me my whole life, I was just learning the nuances of thinking for myself, making the idea of forming a friendship frightening.

I was in a new school, and it was the first time my schedule was split into many classes. That was my favorite part because I was able to dart from here to there with little exposure to the same teacher, peer, nurse, or bully.

The front door bolt unlocked. Stephen was home. His last year of high school was focused on Bible Club, Career Center, and church. Passing me on his way to the kitchen, he said, "Hi," and went around the corner to give Grandma a kiss and a hug. He towered over her now that he was grown. Bending over, he squeezed her as she wrapped her arms underneath his. She asked about his day, and he gladly told of his adventure (at least that is what I thought it to be). He finished his narrative when he noticed Grandma's forearms. Stephen was infuriated.

He knew there was not much he could do as long as Grandma continued to cover up, ignore, and deflect the truth. She did this partially because Mom was her own daughter, and partially because Mom's behavior was reflective of

Grandma's own parenting. She was beginning to realize that many factors made Mom who she was: being a pampered only child, being almost solely around adults her own life, losing both known grandparents and her father at such a young age, and moving often. As a result, Mom never had a chance to become a woman, let alone a parent.

Grandma had invited us, her family, to her home in Virginia to make amends for the shame she held against herself. After we had lived with Grandma Lillian for this past year, it had become apparent that things were not going to change—at least not quickly. So, she reasoned to herself that the shortest way to make things go away was by whitewashing the exploitation and violence.

Mom walked through the door as Grandma prepared the dinner table adjacent to the kitchen. Since her expressions, sighs, walking patterns, face consternations, and emotions often explained her demeanor, I knew Mom was upset

We sat down and ate scrumptious meatloaf and mashed potatoes. It was nice to have a full stomach. Eating, like many other childhood normalcies, was not always an option in Colorado. So, I took full advantage, devouring food whenever I could, to make up for the neglected or malnourished times of the past. I may not have had many pleasant times, but having Stephen and Grandma around brought contentment along with security from imagined or perceived dangers.

Mom ordered Stephen and me to go outside. While Mom and Grandma did the dishes and cleaned up, we followed Mom's orders. It was clear that Mom had something important to get off her chest.

There was no playground or grassy area for kids to play at the apartments. Nevertheless, we had our playland across the street. We got out the nerf football that we had bought on the trip coming out east and went over to the massive green acreage known as the Iwo Jima National Park. (During those days, the park was fully open to the public; today it is only open for tourism.) We played two-man football. I was the quarterback to Stephen's wide receiver, and he was mine. The object of the game was to play defense and tackle the other. The one who allowed the other to score the least was the winner.

After we finished, we ditched the football and became Leroy and David, Private Investigators. We, mostly Stephen, conjured up scenarios, crime scenes, criminal pursuits, and deductive reasoning skills to catch our imagined perpetrator. We had codes, finger guns (thumb up, index finger out), walkie-talkies, and more. It was life-giving fun that I had rarely experienced.

We finished about 8:30, the sun setting as we made our way back up the stairs to Grandma's place. When we entered, Mom was sitting on the chair opposite the couch, where

Grandma Lillian was lying down. Mom shut the TV off and asked Stephen and me to sit at the dining table. My world was about to be torn from the bombshell that followed.

Mom described Grandma Lila's passing and funeral. It was difficult to hear, but my recollection of her did not provoke an emotional response to Mom's news. She talked about Dad's brother and his family. He was now the Trustee over Grandma's estate, which left a small Trust for the grandkids. Mom continued, "In order for us to inaugurate the estate planning, we must have your father's death certificate in hand." I listened but did not get it completely. She went on, "The insurance company informed your uncle that they performed a location search to trace his brother, your father. They found your Dad!" She paused, allowing us to take that in. Mom continued, "He is alive and lives in Olympia, Washington." She was out of breath when she was done.

I was stunned by her words. I sat there, frozen. At first, I was thinking Mom was pretending or making this up, but she repeated her same statement. I was still frozen, much like an injured limb whose nerves are disconnected from its cognitive signals. I was not mad at what I heard, nor did I desire to know the truth.

My brain was blank, except for one thing: I had been lied to my whole life. From the time Dad left, I always had been told that Dad was dead. Apparently, there was reason to believe that he was deceased. The government had declared him legally dead a few years before, and this was what Mom had come to understand. Still, I was devastated by the perceived cover up.

The conversation was over. Grandma picked up her yarn and weaved her crochet needle up and down, darning up one of Stephen's socks that had a hole in it. Mom already made her way to the winged-back chair that sat opposite the iconic couch. She picked up one of her romantic novels. I stared at the wall as a glaze came over my eyes.

I did not comprehend a dad's presence, so I was numb to the information. I did not react to the truth at all. I got up from the table, sat on the couch, and watched television until bedtime. I tried to take in the comedy show, but my mind was fuzzy, a little delirious, and not able to focus on anything. I looked over at Mom from time to time. What stirred within was a rising resentment towards Mom. How dare she keep this from me? Other questions came to mind as the night went on: What was he like? Would I meet him? I really have a dad??

Suddenly, I was interrupted. My wandering thoughts stopped because a rising Presence was now here. His warmth was uncomfortable as it planted itself against my unsettled and erratic emotions. Nevertheless, He reassured me that He was there. I could even hear Him: "I love you, child. Your

Father has always been here." I could not make any sense of what to do with Him, but I was glad He had shown up.

I looked over at Mom as she arose to go to bed. I could still feel the anger I had against her. Everyone turned in for the night. I was already in bed, that steady and sturdy couch, and pulled a comforter over my body that rested on the arm. The television was turned off and I rolled over and pushed my face against the cushion. I closed my eyes. I was alone with my thoughts until His warmth arrived again. I remembered what He spoke, Your Father has always been here. It was not rational, or even coherent; still, my resentment melted at the peacefulness of His words.

I was eleven.

CHAPTER SEVENTEEN

Just in Time

"…Do not worry… The right words will be there.
The Holy Spirit will give you the right words when
the time comes."

(Luke 12:11b-12 MSG)

Stephen was handsome in his blue blazer, tie, and dress pants. At 19, he was attending NOVA, a local community college, and teaching Cobol programming at the Career Center. Although he had been changing significantly from the brother I had known years before, we still cherished each other. He had moved out a few months before, with three young men he had come to know through his church, and his new address was known to us endearingly as "The House House."

I still lived with Grandma Lillian and Mom. Mom was drastically different around her mom. Her violence, screaming, and yelling had diminished. Although her anger still erupted, it was in subtle spurts. Over the last three years of the four of us living together, Mom and Stephen had argued a couple of times a week. She did not beat him as before, but she still grabbed, bruised, and slapped him. The police had been called a few times.

Mom found a different venting outlet. Although I was around, and we had moments of Mom screaming, injuring, and hitting me, Grandma Lillian had become Mom's pummeling, pushing, and slapping victim. The two had arguments that were much more one-way shouting matches. However, Grandma's bruises occurred without other eyes in the room.

The most frustrating part was Grandma's denial of the truth that we all knew was happening. Instead, she came up with fabricated stories, saying, "I banged myself on the counter," or, "Mom was not even around when I fell down today." The appearance of her bruises was such that her stories were not only unlikely but undeniably inconsistent.

There were times we kids talked about calling the police on Mom. We all clearly were still afraid of her, and we did not want to upset Grandma. Plus, there was no corroborating story to match the evidence. None of us wanted Mom in jail, but we thought about ways to stop the violence for good. No one acted on our desire to call the police, at least not within our family.

Stephen had come straight from the Career Center, which was only a few miles away. He visited us at least a couple of times a week, and it was obvious that he enjoyed his freedom and his friends. Since he had been getting counseling from one of the pastors at his church, it had become clear to us that he was more confident and more focused on what he wanted to do with his life. Yet he remained quite sensitive to any physical indication that brutality was ongoing. It was as if he felt the need to be the guardian of our home now that he was on his own.

Stephen had found bruises on Grandma's arms, which stoked his fire. The resentment he had for Mom was at a dangerous intensity, one that had him trading physical assaults in recent encounters with Mom. She was home for the day, so when he found the bruises, he immediately confronted her. I was no longer ushered to a separate location. Rather, this intensifying battle was taking place in front of my thirteen-year-old eyes.

I panicked, thinking that Mom would come after me, which was not uncommon in those heated moments. To avoid attention, I stayed pin-drop quiet and took in the encounter. That meant Stephen got the full brunt of Mom's wrath. She exploded on him after he pointed out the bruising, defending herself by agreeing with Grandma's lies.

Mom had a difficult time staying on one topic for any length of time, but Stephen maintained his focus on the bruising, repeatedly trying to get Mom to admit what had gone on. Mom shifted her focus again, now accepting Stephen's accusations as truth. Trying to point out Grandma's faults, Mom's defense was that Grandma deserved it. However, although Grandma did have her issues, we all knew that meekness and kindness defined her.

Mom's narrative shifts usually reached a turning point, at which she could neither defend nor deny her own behaviors. That is when she would turn to violence as her rage mounted. It was when her guilt wore out her conscience that she turned to a phrase we heard this time and had heard many times before: "The audacity of accusing me."

With those words, she approached Stephen and slapped him hard. She did it again, and again! It was a little comical to watch her as she looked up and threw her arm in an upward motion, hitting his flesh. Stephen kept talking, not letting go of the truth of what he just had heard confirmed: "So, you admit that you hurt Grandma?"

Mom's face was beet red. What happened next is hard to put into words. She started rambling and ranting unintelligibly. It was obvious that her mind was dancing about, trying to figure out what to do, what to say, where to go next, but she was incoherent. She pretended to kick

Stephen, then grabbed his hands and bit at them. She grabbed his chin and put her thumb down his throat. Grabbing his jaw multiple times, she whacked him as he just took it.

Mom spoke long, hard, and loudly for hours. Her language had changed from her more violent rants a few years back. Now, instead of continuing her attack and creating more ways to be violent, she talked much more about Dad, Dan, and Ann. She spoke of how awful they were or had become, endlessly comparing Stephen to all of them, with profuse profanity.

Then, she went on defense, without provocation. She talked about days of old, when, as she perceived it, my brother was in constant need of being punished for "those things" she accused him of doing.

Stephen was more than peeved. The bruises on Grandma were enough to make him angry, but all this malicious palavering was maddening. After all, he had come over to have dinner with us. Then Mom slapped him again.

Stephen riled with antipathy toward Mom. Suddenly, with an open palm, he struck the side of her cheek fiercely, making her head swivel. Mom was caught off guard and lost her balance. By the time she gathered herself, the door had slammed shut after Stephen. He ran out into the parking lot, screaming the whole way.

I freaked out and shrieked, calling his name. Any neighbors in the building surely heard the blistering sounds.

Turning toward the door, I began my pursuit. But Mom grabbed my elbow, in anger, saying, "Let him go!" I forcefully pulled away from her and sprinted after him.

Halfway across the winding parking area, I searched back and forth. I was bawling, decidedly scared that this was the last time I would see my brother. To me, he was the only family I had left.

As I ran down the hill a little further, there he was. I scampered as fast as my legs would carry me. Stephen stopped running and was circling the center of the large parking lot. I ran straight up to him, clinging to him and pulling on his arm. Between my sweat and my tears, my eyes were almost shut, but I got the words out: "Please, don't go!"

The terror within me was horrific, almost worse than anything else I ever had experienced. I thought about life alone, having to face Mom alone, without someone to protect me. I urged him even louder, "I can't... I mean, you can't..."

He abruptly interrupted and looked me straight in the eye. In a definite and determined tone, he said, "I'm going to end my life tonight. I'm not coming back. Take care of Grandma." His scorn for himself was dripping from him along with his sweat.

Stephen's despair fell on me like a wet blanket. My first thought was: My life is over. Although I was concerned about him, that was not as important to me as my own instinct to survive. That was the only lane I could drive in; nothing else was comprehensible to me. So, I wept louder. Stephen, my hero up to this point, told me to "shut up." That was a dagger, and it hurt. I had nowhere to turn. I thought to myself once again: My life is over.

Taking a moment to observe his options, Stephen reasoned out what he would do and where he would go. As he began moving, an unexpected calm came over me. My tears still flowed, but my words came out sharply and shrewdly, "I love you! God loves you!"

The words flowing from my lips were startling, but I kept going. I thought of everything I knew from the Bible, from other Christians, and from the teaching Stephen had breathed into me over the last couple of years. I spoke anything I could to make him consider what he was doing, who he was betraying, and asked, "Is this what God wants?"

When my chattering finally stopped, Stephen was still there. Everything fell quiet. He turned towards me, his countenance had changed instantly. His eyes met mine as he stood still in silence. Then I took the opportunity to plead for us to go back to the apartment. He paused, but he agreed. We trudged back up the hill together.

Stephen stayed for a while before heading back to "The House House." It was clear that something had been altered in Stephen that evening. He informed me later that he saw

Mom in a way he never had before, as a hurt girl, as a desperate child, and as a lost soul. His resentment toward her turned to compassion.

Stephen advised me that I had saved his life. I pushed away that credit when I heard it. I was only glad God had showed up. I had begun to learn that He was there – in every moment.

I was thirteen.

CHAPTER EIGHTEEN

Servant or Son?

"But don't, dear friend, resent God's discipline; don't sulk under his loving correction. It's the child he loves that God corrects; a father's delight is behind all this."

(Proverbs 3:11-12 MSG)

"Therefore, you are no longer a slave (bond-servant), but a son, and if a son, then also an heir through (the gracious act of) God [through Christ]."

(Galatians 4:7 AMP)

Mom found my magazines under my bed, and the terror of what could come next filled me with angst. It was not like it was Playboy, I reasoned to myself. However, her reaction was not what I expected. "So, you want this filth?" she asked. She was incensed, but it did not lead to violence. To her, this proved that I was naughty, insecure, and perverted. She now had a weapon to use against me when she needed it.

Mom was oblivious to the money I usually stole from her purse every few days. It was the first real money I had in my hands, so what was I to spend it on? Junk food? Absolutely, and a lot of it. Furthermore, I had a lot of time on my hands, so I would run to buy actual pornography. I bought it more out of curiosity because I had no idea how the whole sex-thing worked. The more I bought, though, the more I was attracted to it. It became a narcotic and release from the anger and fear that was pent up within me.

Mom and I were the only ones living at home now. In all the previous years, I could avoid confrontation with her. We had some moments of violence, but I was mostly a witness to her unstable brutality. However, watching other's torment did not mean I was not in a state of constant panic. I always was afraid it would come my way.

We moved to a one and half bedroom apartment, a couple of miles away from "The House House." It was strange to not have anyone else around, so it became necessary for me to adapt to this new reality. To avoid Mom, I became an expert deceiver, manipulator, and persuader. I was an appeaser, hoping to make her happy. Yet none of that was enough to deflect the spotlight that was now directly on me.

Mom was alone much more often. She would stay in her room for hours on end, with meals more of an option than a necessity. It all depended on her appetite, mood, or disposition. We ate dinner together most of the time, and then were the times when she neglected dinner altogether. Money was extremely tight.

I spent most of my time in my room—if you called it a room. The half bedroom was an open-ended den that was only separated from the rest of the home by a couch. Watching TV was not an option for me without permission. So, my time alone became my solace. I sat on my floor racing my cars, twirling and jumping on my bed, or having MMA fight-like championships with writing instruments. I was not permitted time outside the apartment, so it became my safe place when Mom was not there. When Mom was home, I kept as quiet as a mouse. I had no friends.

There were cues to clue me into what kind of day it would be. Mom had a repetitive, irritating clap that signaled imminent danger. In preparation for work, she spent many mornings in front of the mirror, berating herself or someone else who was in her crosshairs. If she clapped, added profanity-laced muttering, and repetitively stomped her foot thunderously, it was going to be a long, bad day.

On such days, she usually would fling the door open and follow that with a screaming fit. Once Mom had found her reason—she really did not need one other than to give her an excuse for her outbursts—she then commenced her attacks and assault. First, Mom would grab my jaw or put her thumb under my tongue or in the back of my throat until I choked. When a real opening for "discipline" presented itself, such as a chore not being completed or fingerprints left on a surface, I was whipped with a belt, sometimes with the buckle across my backside.

Mom would intentionally sit on me when I would lie down, making me gasp for air. She grabbed my arms so rigidly that bruises in the shape of her fingers were left, usually on the inner side of my elbow. Slaps were constant. If my black and blue patterns were large or vast enough, she would apply band-aids. As a result, I could not leave the house without long pants and long-sleeved shirts to cover my wounds, regardless of the temperature outside. Whenever necessary, I scrounged up an invented story for an inquisitive teacher or staff member at school to avoid discovery.

When the terror was happening at home, it usually would go on until the point of Mom's exhaustion. After the beatings, she often would say, "Doesn't matter what I do, you just won't learn." That would be followed by her telling me how awful Dad or Stephen was and how I compared to them.

That still would not be the end of a typical bad day. After the torture came, her self-centered, hate-filled monologues about the ferocity of our history and the way "she always had to be the one to step in and deal with it." The past was still very present for Mom.

These lectures went on for hours. How long they lasted often depended on me. If my responses and answers were appeasing and cooperative, then the lecture would last for about two to four hours after the violence ended. If I challenged her, disagreed, or even gave the impression that I had said the wrong thing or shown the wrong emotion, then the lecture would go on throughout most of the night. This often reignited her rage, which led to more abuse.

The tension-filled anticipation of brutality was a relentless reality. Yet there were "good" days—if they can be called that. She would come out of her bedroom some days and turn on her soft rock music. The couch became her friend, along with either a book or a pillow. If she chose to sleep, I enjoyed freedom from the threat of violence, but it was always necessary for me to remain subdued. Waking her from a nap was frightful.

School was better than home, but not by much. Since I was five feet tall going into ninth grade, bullies threatened me, but beatings were rare. What I lacked in stature or friendliness, I made up for by adapting in other ways. I learned to use my tongue to my advantage. That is how I became known as the peacemaker. I could calm a situation down quickly by avoidance, placating, deception, or manipulation. Part of me liked the role of peacemaker because it was an identity I could use. It was also safe. Fear had destroyed my trust of anyone, but it also cocooned me and protected me from danger. Nevertheless, I came to believe that I was unwanted, that I was alone.

Now, Mom put down my trashy magazines. Stepping around the couch, she went back into the living room. As she sat down, she requested a drink, which I promptly brought. She looked at me, speaking as I put the glass in her hand: "I was pretty strong—I mean as far as cleaning up messes. I've had a lot of that through the years. I had to rob Peter to pay Paul—if you know what I mean." She took a sip of her juice, "Out west, things just weren't this complicated. I mean there were misunderstandings, but they got blown out of proportion. They made a mountain out of a mole hill. I don't normally talk like this. I don't mean to complain." She paused as she pondered, "You know I may have made mistakes, but I didn't make them more than once. My intentions were good. I never meant to do anything to hurt anyone."

I was not sure if Mom was reliving a moment or deflecting some shame, but it did not matter. Having her focus off my bad habit was enough to get me to listen to her. She went on and talked about her childhood, her father and his golf designs, the beauty of the Northwest, the Rockies, and southern California. My eyes glossed over. I stopped listening after a while, but I kept my gaze on her the whole time. I sat there for three hours, hoping she did not catch my daydreaming. Then she seemed to wrap up: "I don't mean to be personal. But I have never born grudges. I wasn't raised that way."

Mom looked at me and could tell I was sleepy. It made her angry face appear, so I suddenly became quite attentive. Raising her volume, she spoke forcefully: "I've got enough headaches right now. I have all I can handle!" She jumped to her feet, rattling the wooden floor on her way to her bedroom, and slammed the door.

I sat there in relief, but misery was my friend. I felt like a puppet, only useful for my mom's whims. I went back to my bedroom and threw my magazines in the trash. Laying on my bed, staring at the ceiling, I lamented the waste of a day, or so the day seemed to me. I wanted to fall asleep, but I felt this nudge coming from my belly. I did not understand it, yet I was becoming quite familiar with it.

God came near. He asked me a question very quietly, "Are you who I designed you to be?" I pondered that question, wondering, "Am I God's child?" It was layered with answers. It meant that I had to embrace the truth that I am His, that I was not only wanted fully and fully loved but also fully known. I sighed at the possibility. I did agree with Him.

I considered, "Am I a man?" If so, it meant that I had to embrace the truth that I was made perfectly in His image, made to reflect His glory. It also meant that I had to accept, even embrace, that I was made as a man. It further meant that He was asking me to accept the burden of being made just as He designed me.

I hurt at the realization. It took some time, but I came to terms with the fact that I was made to be a man. My courage came even more. I sat up in my bed and said out loud, "I am man, and all that it commands, as He purposed."

I lay down again in contemplation. "Am I worthy of such a prestigious place and honor? Am I His son?" Everything that I had been taught or spoken over me through the years said it could not be true. Was I to believe that all I had watched, all I had witnessed, all the wretchedness I had become, and all the wickedness I had learned were lies? After all, I reasoned to myself, I had learned to be a slave, a degenerate, a survivalist, and a conceited, self-absorbed, wounded coyote, alone, abandoned, and left to fend for myself and defend myself.

On the contrary, I now was being asked to evaluate the possibility that I was royalty, to be ready to accept what no one ever had put before me, a chance to be a son. I was appalled by my own audacity because I could not bear the vulnerability, the intimacy nor the humiliation that resulted from them.

I agreed that I was God's child. I agreed that I was meant to be a man. Being a son meant I was selected, chosen, nurtured, tenderly held, and the apple of His eye. "No one wanted me," I said to myself, simmering in self-hatred. Even if I knew God had called me His own—and part of me did know—I refused to let myself go there. Even if He showed me mercy, I still felt as if someone owed me more. I pushed away the notion that I was God's son. I could accept being a servant, maybe, but not a son. So, I sat and stewed in my self-pity.

I was fourteen.

CHAPTER NINETEEN

Out of the Fire, Into the Unknown

"He was despised and rejected by mankind, a man of suffering, and familiar with pain. Like one from whom people hide their faces, he was despised, and we held him in low esteem."

(Isaiah 53:3 NIV)

I felt the airplane's wheels vibrate underneath, and my stomach rolled over and over as the pilot took off. I was seated in the very front, by the window. The flight attendants were so attentive to me that it was strange to experience that level of attention and kindness from complete strangers. Yet I understood that it was part of their job. After all, I was only fifteen.

I watched the wing point upward, at a forty-five-degree angle, heading into the skies. Jubilated by the unfamiliar feeling of being free from the people normally around me, especially Mom and Stephen, I was also experiencing deep angst about what awaited me on the other side of this voyage. The anxiety only increased the knots in my stomach as the upward motion of the plane squeezed my midsection almost to the point that I could not breathe. However, none of that compared to the recent events that had led to this plane trip. Resting my noggin against the headrest, I reflected on moments from the last six weeks.

Mom had thrown open her bedroom door, slamming it against the adjoining wall. Normally, when she was this angry, there were noises that intruded from the other side of the apartment, like her creepy hand clapping or profuse profanity, warning of impending danger. This time, I had awakened a moment before her footsteps shook the floor as she swept through the dining and living areas. I could hear her pantlegs squeeze between the wall and the cloth couch.

I had no idea what to expect. With no time to prepare and my heart pounding against its inner chambers, I closed my eyes, trying to pretend I was still asleep. It was the only reaction I could come up with, yet my whole body was quaking in panic.

Every step was closer and louder until I could hear Mom breathe. With my eyes closed and my frame flat on the bed, the anticipation was no more. My torso suddenly bent like a taco as all the air in my lungs launched out of me until

I could only hiss. Mom was sitting on my midsection with all her weight, staying there. Searing pain threw my body into a convulsion. The whole bed bounced downward, and as it came back up, my body frame tried to straighten out. My breaths were short and wispy, my eyes now wide open, staring at her. She had on only her bra and panties.

Everything in me was causing me to gag. I did not want to look at her, but her hand lock-jawed my chin against my pillow while her thumb entered my mouth until I choked. Seeing her lips moving, I had no idea what she was saying. The pain from the weight of her on my stomach was excruciating, and my lungs were hurting from lack of oxygen. However, none of that equaled the dread I felt.

I tried to move towards the wall beside the bed, but her weight kept me in place. She finally relented, removing her hand from my jaw. I moved my chin, trying to see if everything was still attached when a face-full of fist came across my right side. She opened her palm and came again. I could feel my opposite cheek bounce off the pillow She came again and again. Her lips kept moving and the shouting pierced the walls, but I still could not grasp the verbal slander except the words like "Dad," "shit," "bastard," and "How dare you!"

Her "angry face"—forehead scrunched up, teeth clenched, causing her lips to point upward and to the right—zeroed in on my eyes. Her scorn burned a hole through me. With my pain sensors in overdrive, I struggled solely to determine how to get away from this onslaught of sudden torture.

Mom moved her eyes to the floor next to my bed. As I watched, she bent over, reaching for what appeared to be my belt, left on the floor overnight. Her movement was the brief release of pressure that I needed.

Wiggling towards the wall, I unwedged my torso from her weighted grip. Air came more freely then. I kept moving, up and down, side to side. Seeing my movements, Mom quickly became erect, leaping with her whole body onto the bed and onto me. She caught the left side of my ribs, which brought a sharp pain, but I did not care. I pushed myself with my arms and legs until my back hit the wall. Mom threw her backside against my pelvic area that was now fully behind her. I was out, yet, I found myself now wedged between her and the wall. I kept squirming until my legs crept around her. I tried to throw myself off the bed, hoping to get free. My feet propelled me away from her while my head spun towards her in my freedom attempt. In a last lunge, I jerked my body free of her, but my head was caught in her grasp.

My feet were now on the floor. Grabbing at anything she could, Mom pulled my blonde hair firmly into her fists. My face was almost in her lap as I shrieked from the searing pain. Pushing my buttocks away from the bed was futile because it still left my cranium in her control. With a hand on either side of my head, she held the hair at the back of my skull, her grip so tight that there was no escaping.

I stepped back forcefully. Each root of my hair was stretched from Mom's pulling. However, I had come too far to care about the pain's intensity. So, I continued to step back until Mom's body came off the bed. Our bodies moved almost in a dance-like fashion as I went backward, and her feet followed mine. Her hands did not release, though.

Now in the middle of my makeshift bedroom, Mom had had enough of being physically manipulated. She threatened me and screamed profanities until I stopped moving. We looked at each other. Her arms wrapped around my head holding my hair in place. My head pulsated in agony. She lowered her voice and invited me to agree with what she was ranting about. I tried, but I still did not understand what I had done. I nodded in agreement.

Evidently, that was not enough. Mom's grimace turned to a scowl and then rage. Locked between her arms, my head swayed backward and forward. She shook my noggin and all I could do was give in to the propulsion of each wave of seismic activity. Abruptly, she stopped.

I felt her release her grip from the back of my head. Foggy from recovery, I looked down at Mom's hands as she opened her palms in front of both of us. The left palm was sweaty and gritty and empty. The right hand opened slower and more intently. Laying in her palm was my blonde strands.

She threw down her hands, an unsettling cry followed. As she ran from my presence, her bedroom door shuddered at the force of its closing. I could hear her bawl.

I stood there staring down at the floor. It did not hit me until that moment. The hair lying on the ground was mine. I stretched my arm over my head until my left hand was on my scalp. It was empty, gone. There was a void of hair about two inches in diameter.

I was still dazed, but I knew this was not good. I thought about what kids would say at school. I thought about the questions that would follow. My solution was always to cover up what happened in our home and keep Mom from getting in trouble. The more I pondered what to do next, the more I knew I could not hide this malady. I was scared, alone, and without answers. Although I could not figure out how I had an inkling this would set a course of change that was to follow.

I got dressed, left the apartment, and started to walk away from Idlewood Apartments, down Idlewood Road. I headed to the only place I knew to go: The House House. I walked the narrow two-lane road without sidewalks. It was still early enough that there was not a lot of traffic. I arrived at the driveway and walked up the steps to the door. Bewildered and afraid, I rang the doorbell.

Stephen opened the door, and I entered. He could tell I was trembling. He tried to gather information and details, but all I could get out was, "Look.," pointing to the back of my head. He closed the door, turned me around, sat on the chair to get a closer look, and almost fainted. Two inches of hair, roots, and skin were gone. In its place laid a pool of dried blood caked over my scalp. Two of his three roommates were in the room with him. Looking at one of his closest friends, Stephen said, "That's it. I have to do something."

He called his pastor, who had been counseling Stephen over the last couple of years. I could hear the determination on both sides of the phone. Once my brother hung up, a plan was in motion. His pastor became my pastor that day. I panicked at the plan, but I knew it had to be done. He came over to my brother's house. He called Mom with Stephen and me eavesdropping.

Now a quiet whisper roused me from my memories. I turned my head towards the front of the plane's cabin. My stewardess asked if I wanted nuts or a drink. I accepted her offer willingly. It was a nice gesture and I was hungry. With the plane at full altitude at 35,000 feet, I put my head back to rest, the memory continued.

The pastor hung the phone. He was exhausted and a little humiliated by the accosting he took from my mother. He struggled to get the words out, "In all my days of serving, that is the worse encounter of personal abuse I have ever confronted." He finished recounting what had happened. He looked down at my scalp one more time and called the police.

Even though I was glad all this support was here, panic-filled my bones because I knew I had to go back to the apartment at some point. The pastor left Stephen's home vowing that this was going to stop. My brother assured me everything was going to be okay. His calming effect worked. I had thought Mom finally was going to be arrested, after all this time. I stayed at The House House for a few days.

I never intended or desired for Mom to go to prison. I was quite terrified by the imaginative thought. More, I wanted people to be there for me, and this event seems to set that in motion. Mom was never arrested or brought up on charges of abuse. Once I was living back at the apartment again, Mom blew up about the pastor's "audacity to call" her. She wanted to do some physical harm, but the conversation and threat to take action against her seemed to give her pause. The physical abuse all but stopped while I remained with her. For the second time (the first time being when Stephen was bussed to Grandma's), Mom knew she was at her wit's end, and realized things could not continue as they were.

It later came to my attention that Mom and Dad had been corresponding for the first time since their marriage had ended. Dad offered to take me in. Timidly and perilously excited, I complied with Dad's suggestion. So, I finished my tenth-grade year quietly without much bullying from my peers regarding the hole in my head. A few days after school ended, Stephen saw me off at the airport and handed me over to the airline guardianship for the flight.

The plane hummed and the engine noise became a sleep machine. My thoughts turned to the journey ahead. My anxiety about seeing Dad for the first time in my life unnerved me. Mom compared my absurd tendencies and childishness to Dad in her letter to him, saying there was nothing she could do with me. I was terrified and alone again, but I was free from Mom. My slavery and puppetry days were done.

I was aghast and astonished at how fast things had changed in the last few weeks. Now, I was going to meet my father. Sitting in that plane, I attempted to imagine our meeting for the first time. I guessed at what he was like and what he would say when we met. In all my meanderings, only two things connected with Dad: first, he was a stranger; second, I was numb and unattached to meeting him.

"Whew!" I said a little louder than I intended. I was spent after recalling that on the plane. I finally went asleep as the air blew on me above my head.

My sixteenth birthday just passed.

CHAPTER TWENTY
Independence:
Freedom's Evil Twin

"Though he was God, he did not think of equality with God as something to cling to. Instead, he gave up his divine privileges (emptied himself); he took the humble position of a slave and was born a human being. When he appeared in human form, he humbled himself in obedience (heeded and submitted) to God [even unto death] and died a criminal's death on a cross."

(Philippians 2:6-8 NLT)

I walked off the plane, guided by the airline staff. A handsome man of stature waited at the gate, holding up a sign bearing my name. When the thin, dark-haired man, standing a little over six feet tall, introduced himself, I responded with the only words that came to me: "Hi, Dad."

With no emotional attachment to him, I was in wonder of this brave, new world that suddenly inundated me.

It was late when we stopped to get a bite. Dad asked if I wanted Arby's, and I quickly agreed, yearning for something to eat. He ordered ten roast beef sandwiches and then insisted that I eat five of them. I sort of stared at him, taken aback by the feast, but I barely breathed as the sandwiches went down.

My new surroundings came into scope as we passed lush terrain on Interstate 5, from Seattle to Olympia. It was ten o'clock at night, yet the sky was a vivid orange against the dusky backdrop. The evergreen foliage danced past my eyes as we flew down the highway. We did not talk much.

We finally arrived at my dad's home in Lacey, Washington, situated at the base of the Puget Sound, right outside the capital of Olympia. Dad pulled into the long, gravel driveway, revealing a serene scene ahead of me. A barn sat on the right, which I later became very familiar with. Two large stables sat on the property, and the horse fields lay on the acreage beyond, now cloaked in darkness. My eyes were nearly popping out of my head. As we pulled into the parking space in front of the property, there sat a pretty 2500-square-foot house. Lighted by the car's headlights, shadows of the home's facade were strewn before me.

We walked through the sliding-glass front door and then up to my bedroom. Dad opened my bedroom door, which was across the hall from his. He gave me some instructions and told me to make myself at home, closing the door on his way out.

The bedroom felt like a king's mansion. I dropped my things and jumped on the queen-size bed. Stretching out as far as I could, I tried to take in all of it. The overwhelming sensation was too much for my conscious to grasp, but an awakening happened rather quickly. I was free of Mom. I was free of terror. Nevertheless, two elements arose in my new surroundings: I was deeply afraid of everything and everyone, and my new independence overtook everything I did.

Jo, Dad's second wife, was the mysterious mistress who he had left with as I came into this world. She was short and stocky, a little intense, but with a friendly demeanor and a beautiful servant's heart. Every day she got up and made a hearty breakfast, headed out to the stalls where she was the trainer, horse wrestler, breeder, client boarding representative, and much more. She was also mom.

Jo was rarely at home, even though she was usually just a few hundred yards away. Dad was not home at all, except in the late hours or on weekends. He was an independent accountant, yet his ineptitude at handling finances had not changed from his days at the music store with Mom all those years ago. Even though the surroundings said that there was wealth all around, every dollar brought in was stretched as far as it could go. Both Dad and Jo felt constant stress, which meant I was alone in the house for long stretches of time.

I was a scrawny 5'5" teenager, attending my second high school, during my junior year. It was not much different from other school years; I was just a year older, a year from adulthood and further removed from Mom and my childhood horror. My assigned duties on the horse ranch included getting hay from the barn that stood opposite the house, watering and feeding the horses, cleaning my room, and doing my homework. I came to despise the hay job because it was dusty, scratchy, and heavy as I tried to move each bale to the stables, through the constant rainfall or mist that for which Washington is known.

It was the first time I had any type of freedom, and I really did not know what to do with it. High school friends were not an option because of my inept social skills. So, it was breakfast, chores, school, back home, chores, dinner, and bed. That became my daily routine.

As the year went on, my relationships with Dad and Jo did not grow. Rather, they stalled. My independence turned into a child's playground, much like a puppy who comes home to new surroundings and explores his new home by chewing and digging. I was the most upstanding resident in the presence of my new parents, but like that puppy, my curiosity turned into misbehavior, and there were signs all around. I may have been sixteen, but in maturity years, I was a toddler, in the middle of my terrible twos.

The stress of my presence wearied Jo, and she became skittish and unable to trust. Dad would attempt to sit me down after his long days of work, trying to explain the situation and "fix" me. His attempts were futile, as he came to realize. That is when his short-tempered irritation arose. He often stopped in the middle of the correction session to say, "What am I going to do with you?" He then often stomped out of the room, pipe in his mouth and beer in his hand. The rest of the night would be quiet as we watched the small television mounted in the corner of the family room.

As the year wore on, I came to be desperately lonely. It was clear that I was having the same effect on people as I had had 3500 miles away just six months ago. My previous terror turned into devious and crafty displays of random attention-getting acts of nuisance.

On any given afternoon after school, for example, my attention would be on the border collie that roamed throughout the whole ranch. After my daily hoisting of hay and alfalfa, my time became free. I would wrestle, kick, and beat the dog until he yelped loud enough that I became very afraid of someone hearing.

Sometimes my work on the ranch went into the evenings. I typically watered and fed the horses right before dinner.

After taking the appropriate pellets and hay to each stall, and cleaning the stalls if needed, I would finish by watering each bucket. Although I was not allowed to be in the arena or fields with the horses, I was able to watch Jo occasionally as she trained new riders. Afterward, she would usually be inside making a scrumptious meal while the ranch workers took care of the horses.

If the workers were not there, or no one else was around, the work fell to me. It was not a good arrangement because I was as anxious and timid as the horses, with an increased craving for the enjoyment of seeing animals suffer at my hands.

We owned a beautiful 17-hand silver and white painted stallion, fittingly named Silver. Jo's oldest daughter trained and rode professionally, and she and Silver had won numerous awards through the years. Silver was a breeding horse as well, bringing in a handsome fee that helped to offset ranch costs. Yet, as much as any horse, he was nervous and tended to buck if he felt threatened. In some strange connection, I understood that stallion's behavior. On one side, I was desperate to be the center of everything. However, when I was the focus of attention, I bucked and kicked until everyone scattered and ran away.

On several occasions, I turned the spray nozzle on the end of the hose from his watering bucket and spun it upwards and outwards until it pointed at the stallion. The harder

I pressed the nozzle's handle, the more the water's power increased, drenching the stallion. He darted and tried to dodge the weaponized fluid. He hurled his feet backward repeatedly and jumped up and down to avoid being hit. I thoroughly enjoyed watching Silver's prowess cowered by the simple power that was in my hand.

I would look around the ranch craftily to make sure no one was around or watching. If it were clear, I moved on to the next horse, and then the next, until the banging and neighing from stalls and stables filled the air and could be heard from the dinner table. Once I went inside, we would sit down to eat. After constant, unsettled horse movement and danger, Jo would leave the table and tend to the mess I had stirred. She and Dad never found out or questioned me about it, but I suspected they knew.

My place of solace was my room. Unlike Colorado and Virginia, it was my space, and no one invaded it. It was where my obsession with pornography took away my anger, resentment, stress, and panic. It was also the place where I found a Christian radio station. I fell in love with the crackly static that filled my room with sounds and lyrics that rang loudly of the little peace I knew. My faith was not strong at all, but my remembrances of the church time in Virginia with Stephen were moments I came to miss. That radio station connected me back to then. Most nights, the radio churned away as I fell asleep to its peaceful melodies.

Spending time with Dad was not that far removed from his not being in my life for the first sixteen years. Yet being with him provided insights into many of my "whys," offering answers that I never would have known without coming to Washington. I am not saying that my dad did not want me around, but my nuisance behaviors and deceptions brought him to regret his decision to bring me there. They reminded him of days gone by, and the longer I stayed, the more inferences came out about his marriage to Mom and why he had determined that he had to leave. My presence was an increasing remembrance of those days for him. He was often troubled, nervously energetic, analytical, and a visionary, dissecting every problem, with his pipe and beer always by his side.

When I went to Dad's, the independence that I gained became a spirited, rebellious freedom. The more evilness I created, the more defiant I became; the more defiant I became, the more despair and emptiness flowed through my bones. My shame kicked the "real" Dale aside. Controlling my life and circumstances was my one obsession, and the enjoyment I derived from abusing animals satisfied the soul-sized cavern inside me.

The part of me that hated the "real" Dale also came to question why God made me like this. My ire grew as I came to question His existence. What is more, God's constant desire to reveal to me that He was always there, even in the middle of my sorrow, really started to infuriate me. The only thing that kept me hemmed and hedged in is also what kept me trapped from reality and relationships: my incurable and an insatiable need to be wanted, accepted, and safe.

Nevertheless, the radio played its peaceful melodies as I fell asleep each night. As much as I tried to push Him away, God always stayed.

I was sixteen.

CHAPTER TWENTY-ONE
Let It Reign

"If anyone is thirsty, let him come to Me and drink!
He who believes in Me, as the Scripture has said,
'From his innermost being will flow continually rivers
of living water.' He was speaking of the Holy Spirit,
whom those who believed in Him were to receive…"

(John 7:37-38 AMP)

My blood rushed through my veins. As I sat in the passenger seat next to Dad, I could barely contain my excitement. I was surprised that he had said "yes" when I asked him to drive me to a church I knew nothing about, so I was overwhelmed with emotion as we started driving. The ride was quiet as we headed across town, to the other side of Olympia. I had never visited this church, but my anticipation of hearing and seeing everything in this place was hard to contain.

Dad had a hard time maintaining silence. It was clear that my description of the upcoming church service was eating at him, reminding him of something else. He had not said much up to this point as he gnawed and puffed on his polished wooden pipe with the white ivory head. Stopping at a traffic light, he took the opportunity to pull out his good-smelling tobacco pouch and pound another layer of grounds into that ivory head. The match flared as he struck it and swiftly moved it to the end of the pipe in a constant circular motion, singeing the tobacco. Immediately, the aroma filled the car. Then Dad finally broke the uncomfortable silence as he pressed the accelerator: "I don't understand your interest in such malarkey."

I thought about answering his rhetorical question, but he broke in before a thought came forward. His condescending, baritone voice said, "Are you wanting to be one of those creepy idiots that brainwash and distort people? Because that's what this is." He paused, trying to collect his thoughts. Then he went on to talk about a Jim Jones Crusade, likening my one-time desire to go to church—to experience something for myself—to a group of people who followed a man in jumping off a cliff.

As we got closer to the church, it became clear this trip and my reasons for wanting to go was irritating him. His reaction was my Dad's strange attempt at protection; he was trying to keep me from harm. Yet, like most of my family's communication, his comments did not sound as if he were looking out for me. "If you want to go join those loonies and follow them to your suicide, then don't let me stop you!" he said.

Dad's words sounded sour, but I really did not care. My excitement was boiling over as he turned into the parking lot. With its circular structure, warm lighting, and canopy that invited its guests, the building was as grand as the anticipation of the event itself. People filled the area from the parking lot to the entrance. As I opened the car door, Dad tried to say something about what time he would be there to pick me up, but I was out of the car before he finished. All I heard was "ten o'clock." Then he sped away as I turned to enter the facility.

The large wooden doors opened, and I followed the crowd inside. The sea of red carpeting and bright lighting filled my senses. I took a seat towards the back, under the raised balcony, as people flowed in, greeting and hugging. I felt very alone in this foreign atmosphere, but I could only hope that one day I would be around people I could love and appreciate as these people did so affectionately.

I gazed across the 3000-seat, semi-circular auditorium, finding the bright, red carpet intoxicating, while the wooden walls and black-painted ceiling made the room quite cozy. The stage, which was about 40 rows in front of me, was elevated and curved.

Thinking back to my brother's church in Virginia, I recalled a much different atmosphere. Yet it was still a good memory, and I understood enough about church to be caught up in its flow now. Worship was good, and I had practiced enough to be able to participate. I began wondering what I had gotten myself into, but I kept feeling an exciting, yet anxiety-filled feeling that there was more in store.

The pastor of the church introduced the guest speaker, a portly, older gentleman, identified as a well-known evangelist. As he spoke, I reflected on the moment with Stephen on the couch seven years before. Although my brother's had been more raw in his delivery, the lesson was the same. He had spoken of Jesus's death, that it was the ultimate expression of love, and that His resurrection gives us a chance at life anew. Yet my heart was closed for most of the message this time.

As I listened, I concluded that I had already received and accepted this message. I felt anger rising within me because this sermon was not meeting my expectation. My heart was like stone, and I felt I was owed more than this. I had given my life to this jargon already. Where did that get me? I wondered. After all, my life really had been stolen from me, right? My thoughts seemed louder than the sound system.

I participated and smiled at those around me. However, it was a façade. Fear had begun to replace my anger, and I was ready to leave. Yet Dad would not be back for another hour and a half. I started to wonder if he was right.

Then another sensation, a voice from within, quieted my thoughts enough to hear its whisper: "Don't run." My leg stopped bouncing nervously, and I became engaged in the message.

As the speaker wrapped up, what happened next is what I have heard referred to as an "altar call." Two-hundred people stampeded out of their seats to the front of the church. The excitement and bustle were endearing. It was clear the people were enjoying the dancing and singing that was all around my seat. In my spectating, I was caught off guard when someone came beside me and asked if I wanted to go forward, to respond to the altar call. I shook my head. My heart was thumping loudly, and I was not sure if it was because of fear of my surroundings or of the invitation.

I figured the service was almost done, and I dreaded the car ride home. People up front were packed in like seals perched on rocks, trying to get sun rays on their backs. Each stretched out his or her hands toward heaven, and then some fell backward without anyone touching them. It was extraordinary and frightening at the same time. I stood there, feeling as if I were in another galaxy—also feeling emptier and more alone than any at other time that I could remember. Strangely, I knew I did not need to go up front at the beckoning of that call. The apprehensive feelings took over again: Why did I come all this way?

The evangelist stopped speaking briefly before releasing the crowd that had come to the altar. The new Believers that came to Christianity took in everything they could. In this atmosphere, there was a real sense that some were genuinely changed by the faith they professed.

As the evangelist began preaching again, he was targeting a new audience. He looked past the people crowded up front and into the seats, which were half-empty by now. I looked down towards the front. My view had been blocked most of the service because of heads bobbing and hands waving in the air, but my view was clear now. My heart wanted to join, but I had been trained from birth to believe that I was not worthy, not allowed, and not wanted as part of life. Instead, I sat down and pouted, concluding that none of this was for me.

"Some of you came for something more. Some of you have already called on Christ to save you, but you're still empty," the evangelist stated. His eyes seemed to be staring at me. It was impossible for him to even know I was here, let alone for him to be speaking to me. Plus, with the sanctuary still filled with hundreds of people, jitters froze me in place. He concluded, "Well, there is more. God wants you, and He is ready to give you more. Come and join those already in front of me."

My heart palpitated as if it were ready to explode—first, from the panic that struck me like lightning and much more from the overwhelming flood of eagerness about what the preacher had said. Yet I stayed put. I fought the invitation to move out of my seat. The invitation was not coming from the front anymore. Rather, a loud whisper came from my innermost being.

As long as people stayed in their seats, I did not move. The Evangelist urged once more, and people started moving. Then, a herd followed. I started moving without my own consent. I followed the people, even concluding, Well, if they are going, then I guess I will—almost as if I were fitting in with the crowd even though I knew no one here. Inside, my heart was a ticking time bomb.

Standing in the middle of the crowd as people moved around, my body was bumped and jolted because we were tightly packed. I could hear the thumping of my heartbeat against my eardrums. Feeling as if I were being watched, I looked around, but everyone's eyes were closed shut or focused on the stage, watching their fearless leader. I listened more intently.

The evangelist gave further instructions on what was about to happen. Since I could not hear everything he said at that point, I took my cues from the crowd. He kept preaching, and my heart got louder! I wanted to run away, yet I wanted to fit in with the people around me. Nevertheless, what I really wanted was more of this. It is amazing how fear can set in right when the wonderful is about to materialize. At that moment, my fear was at seismic levels.

As I looked up at the stage, there was the gregarious, rotund man in front of me, the one who had urged all of us to come to the altar. Wiping sweat from his face, he encouraged us to be at peace, raise our hands, and get ready to receive something from God.

It was hard to take in intellectually what happened next, but my fellow worshippers seemed to understand, or at least, their hesitancy and timidity were not evident. Music burst through the large stage speakers as the evangelist said, "Now, start speaking as you sing with all your heart. Let Him know you are waiting, and you want Him to come near."

Urging the people at the altar, he said, "Speak! Do not worry if it is gibberish or unintelligible. Just speak! Tell Him how great He is. Worship. And speak."

That is when I peeked through my squinted eyes and watched others. On my right, a woman screamed, pointing her hands and head upwards. On my left, two had their eyes closed, and as their feet bobbed up and down quite noticeably. A few people in front and behind me were not singing anymore, but speaking very loudly, and not in their native tongues. Then, the person in front of me fell directly backward without any seeming cause. I moved to the right as she caught me in the chest on the way down to the floor. Two helpers stepped around me and caught her shoulders before her head hit the ground.

My senses were overwhelmed and all I could do was close my eyes and plead for the same. I wanted it, whatever all these others were doused with. I started yelling gibberish at the ceiling with my hands pushed upwards as far as I could reach. I was caught up in the worship. The gibberish turned to singing, and the words that I spoke and sang intermittently were repeated over and over: "Let it reign!"

This went on for a while as I was lost in this vortex. The speaker came back to his microphone, saying, "Now! Let go and let it flow." I mused to myself, Uh, I think it already has. Yet I continued obediently. What came next is not explainable.

My praising, yelling, and singing had become just speaking at that point. Not hindering whatever came to my lips, I spoke a few English words repeatedly. Although I was fully aware of my surroundings, the atmosphere in which I was caught up seemed beyond this world. I let go and it flowed.

Sure enough, a sound came out of me that was not my doing. An utterance of unknown language burst from inside me. From my belly flowed one word, one magnificent phrase that was not English. I spoke it continually until I could feel my inner man well up. I started shouting the phrase and I could not stop. I opened my eyes briefly to find people all around falling to the floor. A short, stout man was moving among us.

My eyes squeezed shut, I was almost pleading for even more. As the man came in front of me and slightly pressed his palm against my skin, a "kaboom" hit my forehead. I went straight back, falling gracefully, and without concern for my safety. I felt four hands cradle my fall and snuggly lay me on the floor.

The Presence I had seen and felt a few times before was not just with me, as before. He was inside me. Every unsettling nerve and shaky vibration—the constant sensations I had grown up with—was still and in bliss. I knew about this and had heard others try to explain it, but it cannot be told with words. I was in perfect peace, calmness enveloping me. I lay there.

My eyes opened to find most of the people at the front were gone. A few stragglers remained on the floor. The heaviness of being in the Holy Spirit's arms was like having a heavy barbell on my chest. It did not hurt, but I could barely move. I tried to move to the left, and then to the right until I finally was on my hands and knees. I stood to my feet, only to fall back down on all fours. It took a few tries, but I finally arose.

I made my way to the foyer, and out the wooden doors where Dad was waiting. The heavy blanket of God's Presence dissipated until I could not feel it anymore. Looking at Dad as he sat in his car, watching me approach, the emptiness returned. My nerves vibrated once again, and panic settled back in. I got in the car for a cold, quiet ride home. Yet, I was changed from within, a quiet peace resonating. God now dwelled inside me. It was uncomfortably wonderful!

My seventeenth birthday was a month before, but I had a new day to celebrate.

About a month later I was sent back east. I lived with Grandma Lillian for my senior year in high school in Arlington, Virginia. Prior to my flight, Dad wrote a letter back to Mom. He stated how my rebellion and mischief reminded him of why he left my childhood home in the first place. Upon his ending the letter he wrote, "He is so much like you, the very reason I came to hate you when we were together." Mom and Dad compared me to the other, the motive for their disgust, and then both shipped me out. I thank the Lord that He usually had someone there to catch me through my childhood, and this time it was Grandma Lillian.

Through later years, I learned how much God carried me through tragedy and triumph. I learned well how to fear and hate, or how to deceive and destroy others. God was always there. He always caught me, taught me, and stayed throughout. My fear, hatred, and old habits still arise from time to time. What never changes are His tenderness and affection for me.

Heavenly Father always has a beautiful plan, and none of us are out of His sight or His hands. He met Grandma Lila at her old, reliable chair where she would sit and pray. He had an encounter with her as she sobbed uncontrollably after Mom took us kids back home. He made a promise to her—that He would never leave us, forsake us, and ultimately, He would save us.

When Stephen came home from his overnight encounter with his friend. He laid into me that I must embrace this God that I had never known, never knew existed, and did not want to contend with. My soul was restless throughout the time with Stephen, that is until God wrestled me until I came to the end of myself. He came inside and made His home after I asked Him to come. He made a promise to me that day—that He would always stay along with His peace.

In Washington State, to discover this church across a city in a place I was not familiar with, and a dad who wanted nothing to do with any of it—well, that is a miracle alone. I stepped into that facility an angry, desperate, and very lonely young man. When I met Dad at the car to go home, I was changed. My yearning and longing for love were satisfied for the first time. My soul's despair, depravity, and death were gone. He made a promise to me that day—He would always go with me and His peace will always guide me.

In the Bible, the number "seven" has significance to God's way of doing things. It means to make it completely pristine and perfect. When Grandma Lila prayed, I was three. When Stephen led me to pray, I was ten. When God encountered me in a church in Washington, I was seventeen. Seven years between each moment.

He brought peace where others tossed me aside, ravaged and controlled, and left me for dead. He picked me up, nurtured, and coached me through my childhood, and later, adulthood. He was always behind the scenes. He was always the only one left after each ruinous and catastrophic affair. Everyone scatters when tragedy has its day, but He proved Himself faithful time and time again. He stayed at each encounter through my life until I was ready to return to it. He called me to come home, where He was waiting for me.

He called me His son and treated me as such even when I refused that notion. He showed me my own devastation, that which was done to me, and that which I caused. Shame, pity, and guilt burned a cavern in my soul. Nevertheless, He came close, in each instant, and exposed the truth, showed me His hands and His feet, and said this was done for me.

Lastly, maturity has made me understand that my life has been amazingly content. I met my spouse four years after graduating from Bible college. We went into a time of ministry for a short while, and we saw the Lord accomplish and do many miracles. We raised three beautiful children that are challenged with life's circumstances as anyone is, but they are healthy, strong, and able. As I write, I reflect on my fiftieth birthday that recently passed, my twenty-three years of a beautiful marriage, and the bounty of blessings that we have come to have. I realize how different things could have been.

Still, in adulthood, the emotional terror thrived. Being around others was extremely difficult if not impossible. The deep-seated wounds caused involuntary perpetual overreactions and emotional convulsions that made living a roller coaster, rising to a great hope, and then diving into deep despair. Even knowing I was saved from sin and death, I still lived in self-pity and shame. I spent my life's energy trying to get approval, do enough, or prove that I was able and worthy. When I perceived I failed at this thing called "life", an ire and loathing seethed at my very existence. All of this left me empty and fruitless. In adulting, I was even more alone than before. I often stayed there and felt no way out.

Yet He remained. He constantly came close to me and illuminated His presence and His throne. This Man, who died in my place, reigns in my life. He has brought stillness to the terror and halted each storm before it could do further damage. Liberty is replacing the blindness, captivity, and broken-heartedness the longer I walk with my Savior. Freedom from the emotional imprisonment has taken a lifetime to undo, but the snakes that were intertwined with my identity are falling off.

Life is mine and freedom is here. I am at peace. I have a new life. I no longer do those things that held me down have control or have a say. I am wanted! Jesus, the Prince of Peace, the King of Kings, is worthy of every breath of praise I have!

Beloved, you are wanted! He zealously, passionately, and relentlessly chases after us until He catches up with us. Why? Beloved, to show us His wonder and grandness. My friend, to reveal the depth of our wickedness and wretchedness, and the greater depth of His forgiveness, agony, and death He suffered. He has made a way where there was no way, and there is no other way to Heaven. This is it. We must bring everything to Him and His cross, and cry out how much we want Him, and let the Savior come in and take up residence inside of us. Why do you think God sent His only Son? Why do you think He invested all He had in this maniacal journey that Jesus chose and endured? Beloved, you are wanted!

There is a wedding and the Groom is eagerly waiting for you, His Bride, to come down the aisle. He has decked out the halls, brought His best wine out, and stands ready to throw the grandest celebration in your honor and name. You are invited to come and dine with the Peacemaker. He excitedly anticipates and awaits your response to His invitation.

A Perfect Peacefulness

"Suddenly, a fierce storm struck the lake, with waves breaking into the boat. But Jesus was sleeping. The disciples went and woke him up, shouting, 'Lord, save us! We're going to drown!' Jesus responded, 'Why are you afraid? You have so little faith!' Then he got up and rebuked the wind and waves, suddenly there was a great calm [a perfect peacefulness]."

(Matthew 8:24-26, NLT)

The morning had been long as I waited for Mom to recover from whatever was ailing her in that hospital room. Her vitals just were not improving—at least not at a level that made the doctors happy. The pain in her leg, which was the reason I had called the paramedics to her apartment in the first place, seemed to have dissipated at this point. Meanwhile, her body's battle for recovery became more about getting her blood pressure to normalize as well as her heart rate to stop its erratic momentum and to stay in a typical range. The longer we waited, the more the doctors seemed to be concerned. I was aware of what was happening at that moment, but what was to come startled everyone.

A male nurse came to attend Mom. She did not seem to be in any physical discomfort outside of being hungry and thirsty. When the nurse asked if she needed anything, she compliantly responded, "No." He stayed by her bedside, recording what he observed while making his routine checks. Mom took a moment and thanked him for his attentiveness to her, which took them into conversation.

"Well, you are more than welcome," he assured her with his compassionate smile.

She looked at him and then looked at the ceiling with a smile that I had not seen before. "Have you seen the kittens?" she asked.

"Kittens? No, I haven't seen any kittens," he said, smiling back quizzically.

"Well, look," she said, directing her arm towards the same tile she had pointed out to me a few hours earlier. "Warm, fuzzy, white kittens—see?"

The nurse was amused, and he kindly refuted her, "No. I am sorry. I don't see anything."

"Well, they are so cute!" Mom retorted. She smiled at the nurse again. Then, she asked the nurse to lift the bed so she could get more comfortable. The conversation was over.

I looked up as if peering at my Father in Heaven, and quietly asked Him, "What is she seeing?" No response came.

Watching Mom in that moment was nothing like I had ever seen before. I thought about my brothers and sister, and how they would have been beside Mom now. Dan had died a few years ago, Ann lived too far away, and Stephen could not make it until later in the day. I was alone with Mom and had been since we arrived in the ambulance yesterday. I found myself reminiscing about our family's get-together a few years earlier.

We siblings had scattered after everyone reached adulthood, and there was very little communication among the four of us. When we attempted to get back in touch with each other, it was often futile and barely lasted more than a one-time occurrence. There were exceptions to this, such as Stephen and I, who had stayed relatively close throughout the years. However, for the most part, we had deserted each other.

Adulthood had been ridiculously challenging for all of us. Each of us had wanted to end our lives early. A sense of worthlessness, lack of confidence and surety, isolation and desertion, insolence and conceitedness, and the destructiveness of our upbringing damaged our souls and our spirits.

We all projected the same temperament that our Mom or Dad demonstrated in some form or fashion. Somehow, each of us, individually, kept it together well enough, survived long enough, to outmaneuver and outwit the frailty of our own insecurity and timidity, which we all knew too well. Having the Peacemaker, Jesus, beside me daily, in every moment, kept me going. I owe my life to Him.

Dad had died a few years after I graduated from high school. His heart had exploded according to the medical examiner. I guess the beer and the pipe did not go far enough to settle him down. The stress he lived under also seemed to end his life.

Mom's eightieth birthday had come and gone three years ago. Before she came to live with us, she had been on her own, fending for herself. It had been this way for decades up to that point. There had been exceptional moments, but all four children were content to leave it as such.

Mom really did not change through the years. So, a deep-seated need for justice for her actions against us nudged at all of us. It ate at Dan's soul to the point that he had sought to bring Mom up on charges of child endangerment and reckless abuse many years ago. However, it never came to fruition. Inexplicably, there was a tenderness towards Mom in the rest of us that overpowered any need for revenge or harm. We always kept our distance and stiff-armed Mom's presence, keeping her from coming near to our families. Yet we still very much loved her.

So, Ann, Stephen, and I brainstormed a surprise birthday party for Mom's eightieth birthday. We found a splendid restaurant near Mom's home and reserved the whole top floor. Several members of the family attended. Mom had ten grandchildren, and all were present. Ann was there along with her boyfriend. Ann's son and daughter loved their grandmother dearly and showed up with their families. Stephen and his wife of thirty-five years, who had five children of their own, attended. My beloved and our three children, the only ones below the age of eighteen, enjoyed the evening as well. Seeing all of us together was a joy I had never experienced before.

Dan had been invited to come along, but he had declined. He had always yearned to be part of our family, desperately wanting us to come back together. However, his hatred for Mom burned deep within him. He never married and did not have children. The fact is that he was deathly afraid of himself and what he might do if he came that close to another person. This led to a life of isolation and devastation. However, many years into adulthood, Stephen had led Dan to Christ and His cross, and my heart leaped when I heard the news.

The room was dimly lighted during the birthday celebration. Drink stations and piles of presents were around the farm table, which was stained a dark mahogany, perfectly reflecting the soft lighting from above. Each place setting dazzled, the crystal glistening perfectly. It was both intimate and inviting.

Mom stepped off the top step of the staircase with Stephen and Ann by her side. When we all yelled, "Surprise!" Mom was startled—feeling uncomfortable, embarrassed, and overjoyed in one fell swoop of emotion. Her cheeks blushed as Stephen and Ann escorted her to her seat.

We sat and ate, laughing, even guffawing, truly enjoying each other's company. While we waited for Mom to open her presents, I looked around the table and took in the scene of each one's expression of joy. It was the first time we had supped together in forty years.

Jolted by the nurse's entrance now, I awoke from my memories. She informed me that the doctor would be coming in after a while to give me an update and to provide the next steps. I thanked the nurse for the information and went over to Mom's bedside. As I asked her how she felt, I noticed that her blood pressure was still abnormally low. Her other vital signs, though not normal, held steady, and she seemed to be in no pain. The nurse replaced Mom's IV bag as I spoke with her.

As I took my seat again, the memories came back as fast as they had left a few moments earlier. It was the Monday after Thanksgiving. Mom's birthday party had gone splendidly six weeks earlier. The holiday season was getting crazy with shopping and decorating. With my wife and children already off to work and school, I had looked down at my calendar to see what I had planned for the day when I heard Stephen's ringtone. I answered, "Hello."

My heart sank as I listened. "Dale," he said, "Dan is dead." As he paused to let that sink in, I felt a feeling of sorrow I did not know come sweeping over me. I did not understand why, because I had not seen Dan in twenty years. Yet reasoning was not helping! I shook it off and asked Stephen for details.

"I got a call from an officer out of Albuquerque, New Mexico. Dan moved there a few years ago. His apartment was in one of the most impoverished areas of the city, and he was two months late on rent. So, the landlord was sending a couple of guys to check up on him, with an eviction notice in hand," Stephen said.

He took a deep breath and continued, "They knocked and then pounded on the door. One of them pulled out his master key and put it in the lock. When they entered the room, they said the stench was so overbearing that they could not step into the room. The door opened wide enough to find a corpse on an old blue couch. The body had decayed to the point that he was unrecognizable. The medical examiner came back with his report this morning because they were able to get identification through dental x-rays. Dan died of a heart attack. He was 56," Stephen finished.

I was sobbing. Stephen and I talked for an hour. We both found ourselves desperately missing our brother. We laughed, remembering his quirkiness and smile. We hurt as Stephen unveiled more details of how isolated Dan had kept himself. We discussed Dan's last meal with Stephen earlier in the year. I found myself counting back the calendar as the conversation took on a different tone.

"Stephen, when did the ME say Dan's actual death occurred?" I queried.

"Around six weeks ago. That means that Dan's body was sitting in that position on the couch when his heart imploded. He probably experienced no pain because it was so sudden that he did not even move." Stephen stopped his narrative.

"So, he died almost identically to Dad. His heart just stopped beating because it could not handle the pressure any longer?" I asked rhetorically.

Stephen answered anyway: "Yes."

Despite all the sorrow, joy was rising within me. I was praying to Jesus as I was talking to Stephen. I could hear Him whisper, "He is with Me." I smiled.

Stephen was not done yet. He seemed deeply moved by the final revelation he was about to share. There was something in his tone that was different. "Dale… when they took an inventory of Dan's belongings, the last piece of mail was dated October 21st, 2016," he said. Then he stopped talking.

I knew it when I heard it. October 21st was Mom's birthday. It was the day we sat, ate, and laughed as a family for the first time in forty years. "So, Dan likely died the day of Mom's eightieth…?" I tried to ask, but the tears burst out before I could get the last word out.

After I quieted, Stephen added a beautiful sentiment that made both of us smile and agree: "He is finally at peace!"

I jumped now, startled as if I had dozed off in the recliner, yet I was not sleeping. I shook off the memory, although it felt much more like a dream. Just then, a doctor entered the room and gave his update on Mom's condition. He described the dark circle in her lungs as likely pneumonia.

He went on to describe what he thought was happening. "My best guess," he said, "is that the condition she was in prior to coming here caused an infection that has likely gotten into her blood. That is probably why her vitals are not normalizing. Her body is battling it off as best it can. Your mom is a fighter!" I could only agree as the doctor nailed Mom's best character trait. He continued, "All we can do is wait and see."

I listened intently to his words but was not struck by his tone. Over the years, I had learned to trust my heavenly Father through these moments, with an intimate understanding that He had all things in His hands. Quiet confidence overcame me, and my response to it was that Mom was going to pull through. I thanked the doctor for his update.

Everyone left, including the nurses. Mom was sleeping most of the time now. The furry, white kittens that she had described seeing in the ceiling still made me smile but also made me ponder.

Mom had many issues, maybe even some clinical ones, albeit she was never seen for any emotional or mental health procedures. Her main difficulties were insecurity, self-absorption, a sharp tongue, and no intimate knowledge of what it was to be unconditionally loved. Yet hallucination or fantasy was not something she struggled with, even in this moment. So, what was she seeing in the ceiling? I wondered.

I finally moved past that thought and focused intently on her. Praying a little more, I held onto the promise the Lord had given me thirty years before.

I remembered all the times I had beaten Mom over the head (figuratively) with the Bible, the cross, her sin, my childhood, and more. Then I remembered the many times I had loved Mom tenderly, without judgment, without intent for revenge or reciprocation, and accepted her as she was, right where her heart was. I also remembered my painful journey through the forgiveness of her. I remembered that God had given me a promise that she—and not only she, but my whole family—was going to come to Christ, to accept

His forgiveness and invitation, and finally "come home." That promise was a moment when God had come close to me. It was a time when I had been screaming out to Him from my aloneness, out of my desperation to see my family whole and together.

After high school, I found my solace, discovering myself and my direction when I went north to a small Bible college in Western New York, just south of Lake Ontario. The coldest winters and the most beautiful of summers filled the hills of the area known as Genesee County. The school set high up on a hill in a small town of 1500 people, and a school population of 200. Bible classes taught me about God, community taught me what the church was supposed to be, and the love and mentorship I received there taught me that I was worth the price Jesus paid for me. It was paradise and nothing like I had known to that point.

Chapel was extraordinary at the college. The people sang and loved God. He filled the room day after day. The sanctuary, where Chapel was held, was always open and available for students to pray and seek God at any hour. I took advantage of this opportunity, which I considered a gift. The promise I received from God came around midnight on a night near the end of the first semester. I was about to head back to Arlington, Virginia, in the coming days, and I was panicking and feeling desperately alone.

As I sat in that sanctuary for an hour, crying out of despair and anxiety, my focus turned to my family. I missed Ann! I loved Mom and wished she could see truth. I felt for Dan, and I really missed Stephen's friendship. I prayed for all of them. I was young and still naïve in my faith, so my prayers were not great. Nevertheless, I knew I wanted them all to come to know the peace I had come to know since that beautiful night at the unknown church two years before. I spoke all the words I knew. When they ended, I stood, almost whining and pleading, in front of the cross hanging before me on the platform.

Suddenly, I could see a set of eyes and hands less than two feet from me. His eyes winked, watched, and tenderly caressed me. Yet my own eyes were given over to watching His hands. They appeared over my left shoulder in a cupped position, apparently holding something inside them. He moved His hands ever so carefully until they sat right in front of my chest. Opening His palms, a clear, golden sphere appeared, with bustling activity inside the ball. His eyes directed me to take a closer look.

So, I did. There were five people inside the sphere, playing, laughing, and enjoying one another. Their faces came into focus. It was my family: Mom, Ann, Dan, Stephen, and me. I looked quizzically at my Heavenly Father's eyes and said,

"That's not us!" His eyes assured me that they were and guided me to continue to watch.

Suddenly, it was as if His sure hands had lost their grip on the sphere. He tried to catch it and hold it but to no avail. The ball went straight in the air until gravity started its pull. The sphere hit the wooden floor of the sanctuary and shattered into thousands of pieces, including my family. We were all broken and scattered. I cried bitterly and questioned why He would show me this. He did not answer. His eyes remained fixed on me, and I could see droplets forming inside them.

After a moment passed, His hands appeared again, towing a large broom and dustpan. He started sweeping and I clamored for Him to stop. He did not. Reaching around me and the surrounding area, He swept everything and everyone into a pile. He reassured me, but I could not hold onto the hope He offered. I continued to cry until my eyes closed shut.

"Open your eyes and see!" His quiet words quickened me, and my eyes obeyed. My tears blurred my vision until I wiped them away. Then the sight came into focus once again. His hands were cupped once again but in an open position this time. The clear, golden sphere was once again in His hands. My family was eating, dancing, and enjoying one another. Each face—Mom, Ann, Dan, Stephen, and I—smiled as we were made whole and at peace.

The Lord looked deep into my soul, and He whispered, "So shall I do for you and your household. I will restore each one. I will bring each home. Each one shall know peace. Each one shall know Me."

That promise stayed with me as I looked at Mom, then at the machine reading her vital signs, and then back at her. I remembered all the times I had tried to force God's vision to come to pass. Yet I was still determined I was going to see Mom confess Christ and receive Him into her heart. This was the reason I was so sure her recovery was coming, and soon. She kept sleeping, even when the nurses attended to her.

I sat in the recliner adjusting my buttocks to the vinyl's stickiness. Five nurses were in the room. Two attended to Mom's needs. One was there to gather more information for billing. The other two seemed to be assessing the situation. They were the most people who had gathered in that room since we arrived. I was reading, not even thinking about their procedures. All I knew was that Mom was still asleep.

Suddenly, the beeping from the machine monitoring her vital signs began a solid, dull tone that would not end. Two nurses were between Mom and me, blocking my view of her. Everyone seemed to stop in their tracks, staring at Mom or the machine. Then, after everyone had been still for about fifteen seconds, I jumped out of my chair, stepping between the two nurses, and took in the sight before me.

Mom was turning a grayish-blue color. Her breathing stopped completely. Her head laid limp over her left shoulder. She was gone.

I yelled. Looking around the room, I expected someone to act, to start to bring her back. However, before I could speak, I remembered what mom had said, even heard my heavenly Father say, "She wanted to go and requested not to be brought back." I was stunned. It felt much like the shock and awe from my childhood days. Lost and afraid, I stood and stared at Mom and her lifeless condition.

The ICU room emptied quickly. The last remaining nurse spread the curtain to cover the whole doorway. The room darkened completely, except for Mom, the light above her head shining down upon her. It was just her and me. A torrent of emotions flooded me. Really, there were three who stayed: Mom, me, and God.

A love and compassion for my mom flooded me. I wanted to cry, yet nothing came. I had already whispered to Mom the many things I wanted to tell her as she had lain in this room since yesterday. I stroked the side of her cheek repeatedly. Identifying with her tragic life, a life where guilt and shame defined her, I whispered to her, "I am so sorry. I am sorry that you had to endure all of it."

Then an unexpected anger grabbed hold of me. I was not angry with God, yet I knew there was no one else to blame.

I had spent my whole life waiting, hoping, pushing, loving, praying, and believing that Mom would come to confess her wrongdoing and accept Jesus, as well as the punishment He bore in place of hers. I was mystified by God's will, and His decision to take her life. I wanted to yell at Him and yield to Him in the same breath. It was not my place to butt into what He had decided, yet I knew He had made a promise to me.

I was bewildered also. I kept going back to those white, furry kittens. What was that all about? I wondered.

After about twenty minutes alone, for which I was so grateful, the nurses started taking up their jobs. One came to disconnect and remove all the monitoring equipment. Another sat at the computer station and documented Mom's final moments. Another came into prep Mom for transport. Each had her duty, and it was clear what that was. I leaned against the back counter, to move out of the way, and watched the people do their marvelous and unglorified work. There was a beautiful peace in the room, but I did not want to recognize it.

Several workers were coming in and out. Out of nowhere, a lady in her mid-sixties entered Mom's room. She had on the garments of a registered nurse, but she did not seem to be doing any function that involved Mom, her room, or anything else that would constitute nursing. Everyone on staff knew her, and she hugged each staff member as she passed. I was annoyed by her joy, yet I enjoyed her presence in the room.

All the other workers left. The unknown nurse moved around the room as if she were dancing a two-step. She swayed as she walked to the computer station, the back counter, and over to Mom's bedside. She kept humming, intermittently saying, "Can you feel peace in here?" As she moved over to the window side of the room, she flowed past me with a beautiful and calming smile. All I could do was smile back.

Hugging the last remaining nurse, who was almost finished disconnecting the monitors, the unknown nurse made it clear that they knew one another by the affection they shared. She then moved towards the exit. As she passed in front of me, she stopped. Looking up from a height of about 5'3", she smiled, glowing as she said, "Your mom is finally at peace!"

I started to correct her, in that Mom never knew peace, but the woman's words shut me up. Plus, the room really was in a state of perfect peacefulness. Neither my reasoning nor my heart could make sense of the moment. Then the unknown nurse left as fast as she had come. An angel had come and gone.

The nurses could tell I was in pain and angst, so they had called a chaplain right after Mom's passing. However, his arrival was delayed. Then a man entered the room, apologizing for his delay. I did not recognize him as a minister, but all the staff exited the room and closed the curtain. The room was quiet and private.

The husky, well-groomed gentlemen introduced himself. I looked down at his tag which confirmed the name he had used as he introduced himself. It also stated "Chaplain." I took a step back from him, recognizing his authority and position, and thanked him for coming. I reasoned that I did not need him and told him as much. I was confident in my own faith and questioned that he could bring anything to help.

Instead, I engaged in a meaningless chat to accommodate his questions, but I had no intention of opening my heart. I could tell that my heavenly Father was disturbed by my behavior, and He nudged me, saying, "He is here for you." So, I repented of my cockiness and engaged the Chaplain in conversation. I opened up and expressed my anxiety, my struggle with God's will in this, and my anger that He would take my mom now.

His first words blew me away and immediately humbled me: "She is at peace!" That phrase keeps being said, I thought to myself.

I looked at him and said, "How? How could she be?" I hesitated, trying to gather my thoughts, but they flowed easily. "I know the Peacemaker! I know He requires us to repent, confess our wrongdoing, and believe in Him, who was sent for us. Mom never did this, to my knowledge! Every time my brother and I, or anyone else, asked her to accept Christ, she rejected Him, gently or harshly."

The Chaplain stayed quiet and on point, once again repeating, "She is at peace." With God's presence thick in the room, I knew I had to give in. I immediately stopped my cockiness and yielded to what God was speaking through this man. Interjecting my beliefs and reasoning, I said, "If she is at peace, then she must be with the Peacemaker. He is the only One who can give the peace that is in this room!" All the chaplain could do was smile and nod in agreement.

We talked about faith, love, God's will, our right to choose how we shall live, and many more beautiful conversations. The chaplain really was my loving Father's gift to me in that moment. I cried with him, shouted praises with him, and hugged him. He left with that big grin that he wore, saying the same thing that had been repeated several times over the last hour, "She is at peace!"

I was finally at peace as well. Stephen showed up along with my wife and children. For the first time in 36 hours, I left the hospital. I left my mom's side; it was the last time I saw her.

Stephen treated my family to lunch, where I went over Mom's final hours with them. Then we said our good-byes and headed home. As I went upstairs to freshen up, my cats met me at my bedroom door. I picked up the one named Lucy and scratched her behind the ears and right above her tail. It always made her meow softly. My mind still was not able to shake the last hour I had spent after Mom passed.

As I laid Lucy down, I recalled Mom's affection toward cats, especially kittens. She had had so many tales of places she would reminisce about and people in her life—usually the same ones—who left a large imprint and a hole in her heart when they were gone. Yet there was something about kittens that held a special place—a place in her emotional vault, deep in the basement of her heart—where very few things or people could enter. Kittens brought out a light-hearted joy every time Mom was around one or told a story of a cat in her life.

Then, it hit me. She had no idea what Heaven was like, no idea who resides there, other than a place where she imagined her mom was. She wanted God so badly. She longed for the unconditional love that Jesus offers to everyone. I saw it repeatedly in her eyes when she would allow us to have a conversation about God's Son being sent specifically for her. In the end, though, she would push it away and push Him away. Nevertheless, Heavenly Father knew how much Mom longed for His presence even though she could never push through the trials of this life to get to Him.

Yet in the moment that she saw the kittens, could it be? Could it be that in His rich mercy, God met Mom with something innocent and good to take down her defenses and open herself to His true nature? Could something so simple have caused her to see that she has always been wanted? Did she, at the end of it all, finally let go and surrender to Him, falling on His mercy, receiving Jesus' indescribable gift?

Only God knows our hearts. In this life and through these fleshly eyes, we cannot see what God has done for sure. The only life surety and sufficiency for salvation from this world is surrendering to God, receiving the sacrifice of Jesus for our sin and iniquity, and making the Life Exchange--falling on His finished work. "Therefore, since we are justified (made completely clean and whole) through (personal) faith, let us have peace with God through our Lord Jesus Christ." (Romans 5:1 NIV, italics added)

Still, I am inclined to say, "Yes, unequivocally!" Through my faith, the same faith I had when I received the fullness of Jesus in that church in Washington, the same faith that has yielded a close-knitted intimacy and confidence with my amazing Father over my forty years of walking and talking with Him, and the undeniable assurance He set within those words, "She is at peace," said over and over again in that hospital room. I rise up within myself and shout loudly for all to hear, "Yes! Yes! Yes!"

The white, furry kittens—that was the glimpse of Heaven she needed. Whether it was real kittens or angels that she saw as kittens, I have no idea. However, God was calling her home, intimately and affectionately, through His sign to her, the thing that brought her pure joy: kittens. And she accepted His invitation. She is with the Peacemaker, now and forever.

I write these final lines in tears. We never know how far or how wide God's rich mercy reaches. He calms every fierce storm and brings a perfect peacefulness. He wants us desperately!

PGIL2021USA